Dr. Dan's Prescriptions

DR. DAN'S PRESCRIPTIONS

*1001 Behavioral Hints
for Solving Parenting Problems*

by Dr. Dan Kiley

Coward, McCann & Geoghegan
New York

To my son Patrick

Copyright © 1982 by Dr. Dan Kiley
All rights reserved. This book, or parts thereof, may not be reproduced in any form without permission in writing from the publisher. Published on the same day in Canada by General Publishing Co. Limited, Toronto.

Library of Congress Cataloging in Publication Data

Kiley, Dan.
  Dr. Dan's prescriptions.

  Includes index.
  1. Parenting. 2. Child rearing. I. Title. II. Title: Doctor Dan's prescriptions.
HQ755.8.K54 1982   649'.1   82-2360
ISBN 0-698-11175-3   AACR2

PRINTED IN THE UNITED STATES OF AMERICA

Contents

Introduction 9

General Topics: To be read by all 15

Responsibility: Some Guidelines 17 · Getting Off on the Right Foot 19 · Positive Family Activity 23 · Developing Your Authority 29 · Exploration and Explanation 37 · Rules 43 · The Reward of Punishment 51

Specific Concerns:
Alphabetized for quick reference 63

Baby-sitters and Day Care 65 · Back-talk 69 · Bedtime, Mealtime and Curfew 71 · Car 77 · Cleanliness and Orderliness 83 · Clothes 87 · Complaints 91 · Death 97 · Disruptive Teenagers 101 · Divorce 109 · Drug Abuse 115 · Family Dynamics 121 · Lying and Cheating 125 · Manners 131 · Money 137 · Music 143 · Part-time Parenting 147 · Peer Pressure 151 · Privacy 157 · Public Disruption 161 · Runaway 167 · Sadness 171 · School 175 · Seeking Professional Help 185 · Sex 191 · Sibling Rivalry 201 · Single Parenting 205 · Spanking 209 · Stealing 211 · Stepparenting 217 · Telephone 221 · Television 225 · Temper Tantrums 229 · Toilet Problems 233 · Work and Chores 235 · Working Parents 243 · Dr. Dan's 1001st PRESCRIPTION 247 ·

Appendix 249
Index 255

Introduction

We grown-ups face a generation of kids that is smarter than ever before. They are certainly more aware of what's going on than most of us were at their ages. They have startling perception, persistent desires and a piercing inquisitiveness. They also confront a more demanding world where reliable answers to challenging questions are harder to find. They experience more uncertainty and have a greater need for guidance. If you're the parent of an older child, you are no doubt sensitive to the fact that kids face a world that is considerably more dangerous than it was fifteen or twenty years ago.

More than ever, our children need us to guide them in their search for answers to life's problems. But, just when they need us the most, many of us find ourselves torn by the demands of modern living. The economic crunch presses us to work when we'd like to play. The pursuit of pleasure becomes frenzied as we seek to relieve the stress caused by the work. Our need for a relaxed, loving relationship is often forced to take a backseat to the never-ending problems created by the tension of the work/play imbalance. In short, we are so busy trying to survive we don't have enough time or energy to enjoy life.

Our kids get caught in the middle of this vicious circle. While we are busy trying to catch up, our children miss out on the consistent discipline and management essential to their growth. When we see this, we feel worried and guilty. In a state of panic, we seek compensation in extremes. Some of us sacrifice our lives for our kids, attempting to be all things at all times. This only robs them of opportunities for independence. Other parents cope with the panic by turning their backs to the problems and hoping for the best. This leaves children with no guidance, the resulting failures only adding to the parents' pain.

My solutions to child-rearing problems are based on the simple premise that parents can adequately care for themselves and their children by following a simple program of conservation. For example, parents waste considerable time and mental energy in talking, preaching, nagging, reminding and arguing with their children. The saddest part is that these things *don't do any good*. In fact, they usually make matters worse.

I've spent over fifteen years listening to kids tell me what they need. I've combined their explanations with modern research and good old-fashioned common sense to arrive at answers that are both efficient and effective. Parents who implement my advice quit worrying, find relief from panic and get on with the business of raising their children.

I'm one child-rearing expert with my feet planted firmly on the ground. My training at the University of Illinois gave me a solid foundation in theory and research. My seven years as psychologist with the Illinois Department of Corrections opened my eyes to the cost in human emotions and dollars that result when children are left unsupervised. I directed a program that taught kids to stay out of trouble. An independent survey concluded that we were successful with 87 percent of the kids assigned to my guardianship.

My work as counselor with first-year students at a private university showed me another side of life. I learned to recognize the common thread that runs through the fabric of disruption. I learned how minor temper tantrums and other "little things," if left unchecked, have a way of growing into big things.

My private practice with kids and families taught me that money doesn't ensure responsible conduct. Kids, no matter what their parents' socioeconomic level, want rational controls. They may not have the maturity to verbalize it, but they feel secure knowing that someone cares enough to enforce reasonable limits.

My first book, *Keeping Kids Out of Trouble*, demonstrated how my approach solves problems. My second book, *Keeping Parents Out of Trouble*, shows parents how they can prevent problems from growing into big trouble for everyone in the family.

While promoting these books, I had the opportunity to talk with parents from all regions of the country. I heard one message loud and clear. Parents want advice that is practical and realistic. They're sick and tired of professionals giving lip service to things that don't work. Parents know that extremes don't work. They're not sure how to handle the many shades of disruption and turmoil that result when bright, conniving little darlings try to make the world go *their* way. In other words, parents know what medicine is needed, but they don't know the ingredients.

Dr. Dan's Prescriptions will help you find those ingredients. My prescriptions are *behavioral directions*, things for you to think, do or say in meeting the demands of modern-day child rearing. In writing these behavioral prescriptions, I've tried to avoid giving you the impression that one dose of my advice cures all problems.

Most of these directions appear in book form for the first time. A few are taken from the case studies included in my first two books. All of my prescriptions are intended for use by caring parents who want to do a good job in providing security for their children.

In making these behavioral prescriptions, I've assumed several things:

First, I believe that you have unconditional love for your children. This love goes beyond all worldly considerations. It can only be experienced, not explained.

Second, I assume that you are a person who wants to be a rational authority figure to your children. As a parent, you know that sometimes you must exercise power over children's lives.

Third, I'm counting on you to admit your shortcomings. There's no such thing as a perfect parent. You will make mistakes. Admitting them is the first step toward improvement.

Fourth, I trust that you will not give in to guilt, that crushing feeling that results when you condemn your soul because your mind or body made a mistake. Your children need your help, not your guilt.

Fifth, I believe you are tough enough to endure your children's momentary hate. You didn't become a parent in order to win a popularity contest. They will thank you later for loving them enough to be tough.

Sixth, when considering my prescriptions, I'm confident that you will recognize the individuality of the child. Children learn at different paces, reaching certain growth stages in their own time. My advice cuts across all ages and stages and should be applied depending upon your evaluation of the child's needs.

Finally, just as you wouldn't take any medication without understanding its intended effect, I don't expect you to read my prescriptions without considering whether or not they are relevant to your family. For example, many of my recommendations take the form of "things to say" in explaining your actions to your children. I expect that you will change these words so that they best fit your personality and the dynamics of the situation.

These nonmedical guidelines are not to be used in cookbook fashion. There are no absolutely foolproof mixtures that guarantee success. I hate to think of any parent raising children by the book, mine or anyone else's. I cringe at the possibility of a generation of "Kiley kids" running around loose. With your careful and thoughtful application of *Dr. Dan's Prescriptions*, you will save your children and me from that unsavory fate.

GENERAL TOPICS
To be read by all

Responsibility: Some Guidelines

I refer to responsibility throughout my PRESCRIPTIONS. This is my definition of a child's responsibility: *Responsibility is the child's willful compliance with the rational boundaries established by parents in the home and institutions in the community. Or, kids follow rules without being constantly reminded.*

Responsibility Index

If you want to determine your child's level of responsibility, follow this procedure.

- Use four degrees of frequency in assigning a number to your child's behavior.
Rarely	1
Once-in-a-while	2
Usually	3
Always	4
- Give your child a number between 1 and 4

on each of these behaviors indicating how often he or she complies.

$\dfrac{Ch.}{3}$ $\dfrac{Cr.}{3}$

3. 3

3 2

2. 1

2 1

⎯⎯ ⎯

13 10

1. Comes and goes according to my rules/keeps curfew.
2. Is mannerly and considerate of other people.
3. Achieves school grades that are in keeping with aptitude.
4. Successfully completes chores/work without reminders.
5. Shows financial planning and respect for material possessions.

- Total the child's score and keep these PRESCRIPTIONS in mind.

17 to 20   Be willing to negotiate more freedom and privileges for the child.

13 to 16   Keep things the way they are and remind the child that a slightly higher score will result in more freedom and privileges.

10 to 12   There is much room for improvement. You might need to tighten your controls somewhat.

Below 10   Carefully check the first four sections of this book and evaluate your parenting skills.

- Review the child's level of responsibility from time to time (see Appendix).

Getting Off On the Right Foot

Discovering your philosophy of life is a never-ending process. I strongly recommend that you begin the process before becoming a parent. Child rearing becomes considerably easier if you have at least a partial answer to such questions as, What is the difference between the spirit of my soul and the behavior of my body? or, What are my moral standards and ideas of virtue? or, What role does reality, logic and pragmatism play in my decision making?

If you find these questions too confusing or you're already deep in the trenches of child rearing, you need not worry. I'll get you off on the right foot with a few PRESCRIPTIONS that reflect thoughts and actions essential to a parent's philosophy of life. If this doesn't help, you still don't need to get upset. Your kids will teach you all you need to know.

Guilt is damaging to the parental ego. To prevent guilt from making you ineffective, remember that three causes of children's behavior free you from the thought that your kids are at the mercy of the environment you establish.

- Children's unique sets of genes create different dispositions in them with which they approach their environment. These genetically determined dispositions make each of them react differently to the same parenting techniques.
- The environment modifies this genetic disposition such that each child develops a special personality.
- Although limited, a child has a *free will* that enables him or her to complete a decision-making process. If you doubt the free will, however limited, consider this: Children have insight and creativity that often cause them to choose an alternative that you hadn't thought of.

You'd better know what's right and wrong in your own life before teaching kids the difference. Try this procedure for self-examination.

- Write down statements of your values, what you believe to be right and wrong behaviors. For example, it is right to get good grades but it is wrong to fight with your brother.
- Put a number between 1 and 10 after each statement indicating how strongly you believe that your children should be exposed to the information and training suggested by your statement; 1 would stand for "Not a strong belief," and 10 for "Very strong."
- Since you must practice what you preach, honestly evaluate how often your own behavior coincides with your beliefs. Use the same 1 to 10 scale to carry out this very

sobering examination. If you catch yourself cheating, give yourself a 1 on cheating and a 10 on honesty, which averages out to be a 5.5 on the value of being honest with yourself.

You gain a child's respect and emulation when you demonstrate your belief in the statement, "To err is human." So don't be afraid to admit your mistakes.

- Take the child aside and, in a calm manner, admit your error very simply. Don't drag out the admission with a lot of words.
- Pinpoint the exact behavior that constituted the error. For example, "I punished you for breaking curfew while I was still angry. I should have calmed down before grounding you."
- With this approach, you set a good example by condemning your actions rather than your self. The distinction between these two aspects of any person is tough to make. You teach the difference by saying, in essence, "I always like myself but I don't always like what I do."
- It doesn't hurt to add a small dash of humor to cap off the admission: "Wow, that's the first mistake I've made this year!"
- Most of the time, a very sincere I'm sorry is all the restitution needed. However, there may be a situation that calls for you to do more. Check the PRESCRIPTIONS below to decide about any restitution.
- Finish your admission with a resolve to correct your behavior in the future. It won't hurt your authority to say, "Hey, let's both try to do better in the future. Okay?"

Admitting mistakes to older children is tough, especially if you have worked hard at presenting the "perfect par-

ent" image. Here are a few words you might use in changing how your kids see you.

- If your children make fun of you as you begin to change your image, understand that they are reacting to the *old* you. You might say, "People in charge can make mistakes. I guess my biggest mistake was giving you the idea that I didn't make mistakes. I'll work harder to be responsible—just as I want you to do."
- If a child says, "You better not say No, you might be wrong," you can calmly reply, "Yes, I might be, but it's my responsibility to decide that."

There may be times when your error requires more than I'm sorry. If you decide the child/children should have some form of restitution, keep these hints in mind.

- If the child had absolutely no responsibility for the situation and the error was totally of your making, then you probably ought to consider some restitution. However, you alone decide upon restitution.
- Restitution might take the form of an extra treat, an extra half hour added onto the curfew, or best of all, suspend the child's chores for a day and you do them instead.

Positive Family Activity

The key to a growth-producing and responsible "atmosphere" in the home is Positive Family Activity (P.F.A.). We often take P.F.A. for granted, believing that love automatically leads to positive action. Yet modern living puts many roadblocks between good intentions and constructive action. It's crucial that each parent stays aware of family activity, or the lack thereof, and does whatever he or she can do to make it positive.

Tense moments (even days) are inevitable as individuals work to become a family. As long as P.F.A. occurs regularly and Negative Family Activity (N.F.A.) is minimized, parents can be confident that their home provides a solid foundation for teaching moral behavior.

To understand these helpful hints, keep some definitions in mind.

- *Positive Family Activity* (P.F.A.). Any activity in which all immediate family members contribute to a mutually rewarding experience. P.F.A. may range from short and simple (talking, going for a ride) to long and complicated (solving a problem, planting and caring for a garden).

- *Negative Family Activity* (N.F.A.). A family activity that turns sour due to uncontrolled hostility, sneers, disruption, or other forms of nastiness.
- *Positive partial-Family Activity* (P.pF.A.). Any positive activity in which part of the immediate family is missing. This type of activity is occurring with more frequency and includes such things as Dad taking the kids out to breakfast and Mom eating dinner with the kids.
- *Partner Activity* (P.A.). Activity in which a parent and his or her spouse/special friend/ partner engages in an enjoyable activity without the children. For the sake of this discussion, I'm not considering P.A. that is negative and nasty.
- *Solitary Activity* (S.A.). Any activity that a family member does by himself or herself. Your alone time should be positive. If it isn't, consider talking to a professional counselor.

Here are some general hints to be used as food for thought when examining your family's activities.

- Stop negative activity (N.F.A.) as soon as possible. Once you're caught up in a N.F.A., it's best to call time out, back off into some other activity and try family activity later.
- Partial-family, partner and solitary activity support P.F.A. *if* these activities are positive and lead toward family activity.

- Don't force an activity to be a family activity if attitudes remain negative.
- If a family activity has a negative aspect to it (like going to a funeral), you must hope that you have some P.F.A. stored up to see you through the rough time. Likewise, it helps to have a P.F.A. soon after such a stressful experience to compensate for the negatives, e.g., going out to dinner or a movie.
- All family members are responsible for stimulating a P.F.A. Hence, your teenager should be held accountable for suggesting a family activity.
- Humor is an excellent technique to induce a P.F.A. Listen to your children's playfulness and rediscover your own childlike spirit.
- Make it a rule that at least once a week the family does something together. Most families I've worked with find that Sunday is the best day to set the stage for P.F.A.
- If you have trouble inducing a P.F.A., begin by increasing your P.A. and P.pF.A. This way you establish a base of good feelings upon which to build successful P.F.A.

There are thousands of inexpensive things you can do to induce a P.F.A. Here are just a few:

- Go to the library on the weekend and review the latest magazines, encourage kids to learn about new hobbies, listen to music or have the children hunt for the value of collector items you have around the house. Discuss the outing in the car coming and going.
- Get bicycles for everyone (buy used ones at police auctions) and start a group exercise program.
- Help the children learn how to cook, and

have one day when the whole family prepares the meal.
- Divide up a cleaning project around the home and have everyone participate at the same time.
- With a little planning, even grocery shopping can be a P.F.A., provided each family member has a job.

Coping with negatives during a family activity is tough. If you don't want to call time out (or can't), consider these PRESCRIPTIONS.

- To express your anger constructively, try this: "I'm mad at you right now because you won't help the family with this problem."
- Ignore nasty comments and completely change the subject.
- Make a side comment that might encourage the nasty one to change his or her attitude. For example, say to your spouse, "I sure wish Sarah (Billy) could join us in this activity and not be so negative."
- Remember to start any direct comment with the word "I," not "You." For example, instead of saying, "You just like to see me suffer," say, "I feel bad when you attack me like that."

It's fine to involve other people in your family's activities. But allow some room for P.F.A.

- Permit the kids to participate in another family's activity or other kids in yours, but equalize these activities with P.F.A.
- Family activities that include relatives not members of the immediate family tend to detract from P.F.A. If a relative lives with

you, find time to enjoy positive activity with immediate family members only.

If you are a single parent, you can still enjoy P.F.A.

- A single parent and his or her child/children constitute the immediate family.
- Single parents have to expend more time and energy stimulating a P.F.A. and quickly disciplining any disruption. So pay special attention to the hints about coping with negatives outlined above.
- If you have a special friend or future spouse involved in activities, assure yourself of the permanence of your new relationship before including that person in everything you do. My view is that, once you make a commitment to a new partner, the activity between you and the kids should include that other person. You are working with a new family and you should give the kids time to adapt.

One last thing to keep in mind:

- Don't spend too much time analyzing or diagramming the activity in your home. More often than not, S.A., P.A., P.pF.A., N.F.A. and P.F.A. occur in rapid-fire, random succession. Always trying to figure it out may cause you to miss the opportunity to engage in a P.F.A.

Developing Your Authority

A parent's primary job is to be a responsible authority figure. No matter how well you train yourself, there will always be more to learn. Your authority develops as you and the child grow together. Developing authority calls for you to find the happy medium between two equally important duties. You must balance rights with responsibilities, time for your kids with time for yourself, your Nos with your Yeses, anger at disruption with love for the child's uniqueness, and meaningful discussion with unilateral decisions.

It's very easy to lose your balance. Sometimes you're too tired to give your kids the time they need. Extremely disruptive children can cause you to dig yourself into a hole where you're constantly saying No. And finding the right time to cut off a discussion and make a decision that will stick can severely tax your self-confidence.

Parents who fail to develop authority are often caught up in wondering Who's in charge here? If this is happening to you, then I suggest that the answer to this question is, Nobody.

Here are some PRESCRIPTIONS that will help you develop your authority so that you can maintain your balance.

As you may know by now, my position is that children must be given some orientation to responsibility. To separate the responsibility of the parent from that of the child, repeat this guideline to yourself and your kids.

- I don't blame myself when my children goof up, they are at fault. However, I do blame myself if I don't do something about it.
- Or try this one: My kids have rights. I need to help them learn how to be responsible so that they can protect their rights.

The best time to start developing responsibility in a child is early in his or her life. Here's one thing that you can do to help a toddler learn responsibility.

- Have the child repeat your instructions as you help him or her follow through on those instructions. Thus, when you tell your child to "Pick up the toys," walk the child through the task as you prompt the child to say, "Pick up the toys."

Following through on your directives is essential. This can be tough when you're boxed in—love on one side, the kid's disruption on the other. Following through can be as easy as one, two, three.

1. The first step is the giving of a simple instruction, such as, "Take out the garbage please." Don't give an instruction if you

don't intend to take the next two steps.

2. If the child doesn't do as instructed, the next words out of your mouth should take the form of a warning: "If you don't take out the garbage, you will be punished." (Specify the punishment if the child doesn't already know what to expect.)

3. Allow a reasonable amount of time for compliance, say two or three minutes. Then, without any further talk, take the action you indicated in the warning.

Saying No isn't as easy as you might think. Here are a few hints that make saying No a bit easier.

- Don't be too sweet when you say No. If you're smiling and trying to be warm while giving a negative response, your child will get mixed messages. If you're going to say No, say it sternly and flatly so that your child knows that it's time to shape up.
- As much as possible, move your toddler when you say No. For example, when you say No to playing with your vase, move the child's hand away from the vase as you say No. This way, your child gets the message that No means movement.
- Don't say "I'll think about it" when you actually mean No. You might think this is a good tactic, but it only opens the door for arguments and complaints.
- Rules provide excellent guidelines for saying No. Check the chapter entitled "Rules" and you'll see ways to reduce the hassle of saying No.

The older your child becomes, the more you should

attempt to reduce your words when saying No. Your authority takes on more meaning if you can give nonverbal signals indicating No.

Here are a few ways to say No without opening your mouth.
- Look directly at the child while he or she is being disruptive and shake your head from side to side.
- Or, while looking at the child, snap your fingers to gain his or her attention and then wave your finger back and forth.
- Turn stone faced and silent and just look sternly at the child until he or she quits the disruption. This "evil-eye" maneuver should be coupled with shaking your head from side to side the first few times you use it.
- You can use any combination of these or other nonverbal signs to reduce the amount of talking you have to do when confronting a problem. One of my favorite guidelines is this: When giving a penalty, try to keep your words under fifteen. For example, "You forgot your chores. So you may not watch TV after dinner."

If you behave in a responsible manner, trust, admiration and emulation are just a few of the wonderful by-products. But what about fear? Healthy fear should evolve as you develop your authority.

- In order to avoid guilt and worry, remember this definition of healthy fear: Fear is healthy when it occurs *after* children have done or thought about doing something *that they know is wrong.* Healthy fear protects children by causing them to avoid behavior that is harmful. Fear is healthy when kids fear a punishment; it is unhealthy if they fear losing your love.

- Separate your love from your praise and punishment. This enables you to reject a child's behavior without rejecting the child. Here's a thought that might help: I will try to find the best way to deal with your disruption. But I'll never quit loving you.
- To keep fear under control, be stern, keep the penalty brief and return to a pleasant attitude after fifteen or twenty minutes.
- Since fear needs to be balanced by positive feelings, I suggest this: Give the child many opportunities to engage in activities in which he or she can gain a strong dose of honest pride. That way, children learn to fear things that can get them into trouble and to have pride (and brag a little) about things that keep them safe. The Merit/Demerit Chart (see Appendix) will help you develop the positive and negative aspects.
- When your children are older, say school age, explain fear this way: "I want you to fear what bad things could happen to you if you behave recklessly. I want red lights to flash in your head *before* the red lights of an ambulance or police car start flashing."

Just because your children are happy and healthy, don't expect them to accept your Nos without occasional defiance. When kids protest your No, grab hold of your authority and hang on.

- Once you've engaged in open discussion, you should make the best decision you can; don't argue about any Nos.
- Follow the example of a referee and hold your hands in the form of a **T**, indicating

"time out." Shake your head from side to side the first time you use the **T**, indicating that the sign means, "Stop your protest and go to a neutral corner."

- If you know that the child knows your reason for saying No, don't be afraid of shutting off protests by holding your hands in front of your face, palms toward the child, in effect saying, "This conversation is over."

Developing authority means overcoming childish manipulations. Although you won't win them all, here are some coping comebacks that will help you survive the situation in which children ask for something that is obviously against the rules.

- Ask them in return, "Can you tell me why I must say No?"
- Or answer their question with this question, "Why are you trying to make me go against my own rules?"
- Or put the responsibility on their shoulders with this question, "What is the house rule about _____?" (Specify the issue.)
- Keep a smile on your face when you reply, "Why don't you tell me what my answer will be?"
- You can change the subject by getting to the heart of the issue when you say, "Wow, you sure must want to argue today. What's bugging you?"
- Whether you use one of my PRESCRIPTIONS or not, stick to your guns. If it's against the rules and there's no room for exceptions, don't bend the rules!

There are times when you will decide to change your

mind. That's okay. Just don't do it because of defiance. That sets you up to be blackmailed.

- Always be looking for new information affecting the rules you make. I hope that some of my PRESCRIPTIONS will cause you to change your rules in a constructive manner.
- You may decide to grant an exception to the rules when the child accepts your No without defiance. You can explain that you are permitting an exception because the child demonstrated maturity by not arguing. You can always change your mind.
- If the rule is negotiable (see the chapter on Rules) and the child has shown responsibility, you can change your mind.

Sometimes discipline becomes so taxing that you forget to give the child Yes experiences. Here are a few hints to help you remember that the little things often count more than you expect.

- Say, "I appreciate that" when the child remembers his or her chores without being constantly reminded.
- Give the child a small treat when he or she waits patiently while you complete a boring job or activity (waiting in a doctor's office).
- Don't forget to give lots of hugs, pats and kind words when kids help you without being asked.
- You can say Yes to an extra half-hour of television when your child gets a good grade on a tough test.

Exploration and Explanation

Kids see things in black and white. When they explore their world, they look for simple, clear-cut answers. When they are younger, they automatically turn to their parents for explanations of their experiences. As they grow older and gain independence, they become choosy about whom they trust for guidance. If you want your explanations to have a meaningful impact on your kids, it is crucial that you retain credibility.

You develop credibility by being a firm, gentle and responsible authority figure. If your behavior supports your values and vice versa, you give your children a solid foundation to relate to. Even though they won't always agree with you, they'll always be interested in hearing what you have to say.

The toughest part of an explanation is not *what* to tell the children, but finding out what they need to know. You can unlock this door to information by always respecting your children's experiences. Let the kids know that while their experiences may be misleading, misdirected or just plain incorrect, they are never "bad." All experiences are good, if for no other reason than that the child had them and the child is essentially good. This core of internal "okayness" is absolutely necessary for the further development of a healthy child.

It's very tempting to give over-simplified answers to complicated questions. Yet, if you do, your credibility suffers. Keeping it simple is fine, but answer the question honestly.

- When children ask difficult questions, you first must find out exactly what they're asking. If your child asks, "Why do friends fight?" respond, "Tell me when you've seen friends fight." Or, "Did you have a fight with your friend?" This helps you pinpoint a situation so that you and the child will be talking about the same thing.
- Once you know what the child is asking, give your answer in a manner that minimizes prejudice and encourages further discussion. Introduce your remarks by saying, "My opinion is that . . ."
- If you don't know the answer to a question, tell the child that you don't know but will find out.

When children explore their world, it is inevitable that they will cross the limits you've established. Disruption has a silver lining.

- You can take some solace in the fact that healthy, bright kids *should* test your limits. If they don't, count your blessings and hold on, they might still.
- If they do, you can take pride in the fact that children who feel secure with your love will

38

be the first ones to see how far you'll let them stray.
- Enjoy yourself. Watching your beautiful offspring concoct all sorts of manipulations can keep you young at heart.

Although maddening, testing the limits can be viewed as a "good" experience. While you shouldn't yield to the manipulations, there's no reason you can't recognize the child's creativity. Here are a few responses to disruptive explorations.

- "Nice try, honey, but you still have to do as I said."
- Or, "Boy, you almost had me that time. That was a pretty slick move. Now do as I said."
- Or, "I'm sorry that I can't let you break the rules. That con job was a very smart move."

The role that best enables you to influence your children's exploration is that of guide. You may know what lies ahead, but resist the temptation to tell your children what to experience.

- Help your children become aware of their own thoughts at an early age. When they are experiencing a piece of life, ask them, "What does your brain say to you about _____?" (the situation).

Following this self-reflection, encourage children to make a choice, no matter how simple.

- Give young children a choice of two toys during bathtime by saying, "Which toy do you choose to play with?"
- Help older children cope with complicated

situations by outlining their dilemmas. For example, to a teenager you might say, "You seem to have a problem. On the one hand you really like that boy (girl) and would like to date him (her). On the other, if you hope for a date, you run the risk of him (her) not liking you. Tough choice!"

As a parent and guide, you sometimes must state your authority by limiting the alternatives the child has available to choose from.

- Very matter-of-factly, say, "You do not have the choice of going to that party unchaperoned. However, you may have the party here or show me that other responsible adults will supervise the get-together."

You can give toddlers an increased sense of responsibility during their exploration by discriminating among three types of experiences.

- The very expensive, fragile, "adult" things can only be looked at.
- Other "grown-up" things can be touched but not played with.
- Finally, there should be many things that *can* be played with.

Learning a new job is tough for all of us. Excited, pleasure-seeking children are no exception. Follow these PRESCRIPTIONS *when explaining a new job.*

- Be specific. Tell the child exactly what to do.
- Demonstrate the job, especially the difficult parts.
- If the child is confused or has a bad memory,

have him or her write the explanation down on a piece of paper.

- Supervise the child's first try at the new job. Keep your remarks positive and constructively critical.

Many parents get themselves into trouble by overdoing explanations. Once you know that your children know what to do, follow these hints.

- Don't argue about the refined points of any job.
- Avoid any power struggle with a child who is forgetful or lazy. If you engage in a power struggle, you are admitting that you're not sure about what you asked the child to do.
- If children's complaints cause you uncertainty, review your explanations in your own head and consider starting fresh.
- If you decide that your child deserves an answer to why, use yourself as a reference point. Rather than referring to another person's viewpoint, let the child know that you, as an informed adult, have the final word.
- When a new situation suddenly crops up, try to explain a negative answer *before* saying No to the child.
- If that's not possible, explain your response after the child has accepted the No and things have quieted down.
- Don't explain your No right after saying it. Children hearing a No are rarely in a rational mood.
- If challenges continue, ask, "What more do you need to know?"

Rules

If you're familiar with the child-rearing books of the past twenty years, you're not surprised when I summarize their advice this way: Authority hurts kids, power interferes with growth space, and, by all means, children need space to grow.

I agree that children need growth space. However, I disagree with the implication that this space should be unlimited. No rules is just as harmful as too many rules. I don't like either alternative. Somewhere between the two extremes lies the happy medium of rational rules.

Rules act as out-of-bounds markers, guiding children as they play the game of life. Giving children no rules is the same as permitting athletes to play sports with no penalties. In both cases, chaos results and disorder becomes the order of the day.

Children feel secure when they know the boundaries of the space in which they may safely experiment with finding themselves. To give them this security, parents must exercise power in establishing and enforcing the boundaries that are laid down by rules.

There's another important reason children should have rules. It is something that many people forget about; that is, parents need space too, space to have time to themselves, space to enjoy leisure activities and space within which they feel confident about their child-rearing efforts.

The following PRESCRIPTIONS should help you set rules that give kids space to develop their skills while providing you with the space to enjoy the life that you've worked so hard to attain.

If you want to proceed step by step in setting and enforcing rational rules, the first thing you need to do is make a list.

- Encourage your kids to think about the current rules and write down suggestions for changes that pertain to their wishes. Listen to your children's ideas but let them know that you have final approval over the rules.
- Separate your rules into two categories, negotiable and nonnegotiable. The major difference is that you won't be willing to compromise on nonnegotiable rules. See the section below that pertains to the difference between the two types of rules.
- State your rules so that the children know exactly what is expected of them. For example, rather than say, "Do your chores," say, "Clean up your bedroom, take out the garbage and do the dishes." To avoid confusion, you might wish to write the rules down on paper.
- Furthermore, you can minimize future hassles by requiring that the kids post individual copies of rules that pertain to them in a

prominent place, say the kitchen or the bedroom.

- You must face the fact that you can't be all things to your children all the time. Accept this reality by ranking your rules in some order of importance, Here is my PRESCRIPTION for a sample list of rules for a 10-year-old:
  1. Check in by 4 P.M. and be home by 5:45 for dinner.
  2. Complete all homework before watching TV.
  3. Clean bedroom, empty garbage and feed the dog daily.
  4. Display good manners at home and school.
  5. Do special household jobs to earn spending money.

Given the limitations on your energy, concentrate your work on implementing these rules, not arguing over them. Use the chart in the Appendix for help.

Don't worry about getting your list exactly right the first time. Rules are meant to grow and change as children mature. So, like Santa Claus, once you make your list, check it twice (at least).

- Set aside some time on a regular basis to review the rules in a quiet, calm atmosphere. I usually recommend Sunday evening.
- Encourage the children ahead of time to bring their ideas in written form so that they won't forget what they want to say.
- Make sure you keep the responsibility on the kids by saying, "These rules are for your benefit, so speak your piece. Once they are in effect, I won't talk about them."
- Permit the kids to complain about the rules

during this quiet discussion. But help them understand that you must still make the decisions, many of which will not be popular.

- By the end of the discussion, you should have deleted any rules that you haven't been able to enforce and changed rules that proved to be confusing or ambiguous.
- Ask the kids for their ideas on improving your rewards and punishments. Keep in mind that they may think that $100 is a good reward and that flogging is an excellent punishment.

Rules don't have to be the growling threats of parental monsters. They can be one way you express your protective love for your children. So, once you make your list and check it twice, don't forget to find out who's naughty and nice.

- Here's my number one rule about making rules: Don't make a rule you can't or won't enforce.
- You can keep your self-confidence and minimize hassles by tying all rewards and punishments to behavior that conformed to or violated the rules.
- Your rules become matter-of-fact if you make a brief mention of the compliance or violation as you give out the reward or punishment. Hence you say, "You can have an extra dollar to spend because you helped me clean the garage without being told twice." Or, "You lose an hour of television tonight because you were late getting home from school."
- Remind children that they can advance to more lenient rules and greater privileges

after they demonstrate that they can successfully comply with current rules.
- If one child makes fun of another child's penalty, that child gets a penalty also.

Nonnegotiable rules should be part of house rules. These are made by the parents without discussion.

- These rules should be stated *before* any discussion of rules by saying, "As parents, we must make some rules that are not open to change. Don't waste your time getting upset about these rules. It won't do you any good."
- Keep your nonnegotiable rules to a minimum, say three or four.
- Examples of nonnegotiable rules would be:
  1. There will be no illegal activities under this roof.
  2. You will not be free to come and go as you please.
  3. You will show respect through good manners.
- Violation of nonnegotiable rules *always* results in some form of disciplinary action. You *never* grant an exception to these rules.

Negotiable rules dominate your rules as they permit both parent and child great flexibility.

- Be willing to negotiate any area in which the child has demonstrated that he or she is responsible. Hence, you say, "I'll consider letting you watch that TV program tonight because you have really improved in getting along with your brother."

- You can reduce some of the hassle by stimulating compromise. You can say, "I will have the final say so try to think of a rule that I can allow. I really don't like saying No. Help me out."
- Parents must remain the final judge after the negotiations have taken place. Try your best to explain your position, but don't back down just because a child still doesn't accept your explanation. Maintain your authority.
- Examples of negotiated rules might be:
    1. "If you get a B on the English test you have this week, I'll extend your curfew one hour this weekend."
    2. "You can watch that program on TV next week only if you show me that you can control your temper." (This might apply if the program had some violence in it.)
    3. "You can buy that special pair of designer jeans after you put 20 percent of the money you earned into a savings account."

Many parents wonder about treating everybody equally. Give your children a lesson in reality. "Rank has its privileges," but keep your eye on justice when you give this lesson.

- Like it or not, there are times when you must reserve the right to say No and give no explanation. This is true because sometimes you must make the judgment that the situation is beyond a child's comprehension and therefore he or she should simply obey. An example of this might be when you are attending a family gathering and weird Uncle Charley gets too much to drink and you know that, within fifteen or twenty minutes, he and his wife, along with Great Aunt Minnie, will get into a knock-down-drag-out fight, complete with extensive cussing and swearing. Even though the children are playing happily with their cousins, you tell them that you are leaving early. They complain, whine and argue. At a moment like this, you must pull rank and say, "We're going!" You can explain your actions later.

- Younger children must also learn how to deal with rank, in that older siblings should have more freedom and privileges.
- Don't hesitate to pull rank yourself sometimes. You don't always have to eat at Hot Dog Heaven just because the kids want to. Or you may want to watch a certain program on television, which means the kids don't get their first choice.

As you give your children lessons in the reality of living, don't forget to balance the harshness. Hence, while rank has its privileges, it also has its price.

- The more often you pull rank on your children, the greater the likelihood that they will eventually rebel against a harsh dictatorship. So don't pull rank very often and, when you do, take time later to explain how and why you did it.
- If older children enjoy more privileges, they should also shoulder the burden of greater responsibilities. In effect, they get more but they have to work harder.

The Reward of Punishment

Many parents are beseiged with guilt when they punish their children. "Oh, I'll harm him," or "Will she forgive me?" or "What if I damage his psyche?"

Punishment doesn't have to be a dirty word. In fact, if you learn the correct procedures, your children will learn from their mistakes. Then you don't have to repeat the punishment very often. If you start punishments off on the right foot, you can reduce them to a minimum or even eliminate them, *provided* your children cooperate with you.

I find that parents who have trouble with continually disruptive children usually don't punish correctly. They yell and scream when they ought to take firm action. They time their punishments such that the child doesn't understand why he or she got punished, or they punish so harshly that rebellion is stimulated. When punished incorrectly, the kids don't see the connection between the misbehavior and the penalty. In turn, they see you as mean and miss the entire point of the punishment.

Punishments are tough to give as well as receive. If done properly, they prevent future disruptions and promote self-control. Children need self-control in order to successfully adjust to a demanding world. Thus rational punishments give your children a gift that they can use their entire life. *This is the reward of punishment.*

Consider these PRESCRIPTIONS for learning how to make punishment work for you and your children.

Parents often get the impression that discipline means punishment and punishment is bad. Not so!

- Discipline means "to teach." Rewards are just as important as punishments, even more so. Use both in teaching right from wrong.

Because loving parents don't like to punish their children, they often stumble over the words to use when initiating penalties. Here are a few things to say when you explain why you use punishment.

- "You still need to be parented, don't you? Well, I can't be your parent and look the other way when you misbehave."
- "I don't expect you to love the penalty. If you're unhappy, that's okay."
- "The best way to reduce the hassle of punishment is for you to just accept the penalty and get it over with."

The restriction of freedom, or "grounding," is a powerful punishment. However, it loses its effectiveness very quickly if not done properly. Follow these hints in carrying out grounding.

- Grounding can occur in stages or degrees.
  1. *First degree:* Grounded to the yard. Friends may come over.

52

2. *Second degree:* Grounded to house after dinner; no friends.
3. *Third degree:* Grounded to house after school; no friends.
4. *Fourth degree:* Grounded to house for entire day except for school.
5. *Fifth degree:* Grounded to room for a specific time period when not attending school.

- Use grounding only if child can be supervised the entire time.
- Keep grounding to a short period of time. Increase the degree of grounding rather than the length of time. Don't ground your child for more than one week at a time. Otherwise, you end up punishing yourself more than the child.
- All exceptions to the grounding are granted by a responsible adult for a specific purpose. For example, grounding might be lifted for a short period while the child is doing school work, attending a job or an activity relating to his or her duties.
- If, under dire circumstances, you decide to suspend the grounding, make the child do an hour or two of work to compensate for the suspension of grounding.

An excellent form of control is "time out." Time out often doesn't work because it isn't done correctly. Standing in the corner or sitting on a chair are two good forms of time out.

- Standing in the corner or sitting on a chair employs boredom as a penalty. You reduce the attention you give the child by using a kitchen timer to time the length of the boredom.

- When placing the child in the corner or on the chair, say, "You are to stay here for _____minutes without making any noise. You are free when the bell rings." Start with the number of minutes that the child is old. Thus a 5-year-old stands or sits for five minutes. You might double the number of minutes if the original penalty doesn't work. If double the minutes still doesn't work, find another solution.
- If the child won't stay in the corner or on the chair (which will probably happen the first time you try it), you must gently but firmly hold him or her there saying, "Your time will start when I let go of you and you stand (sit) still and say nothing."
- If the child creates a fuss halfway through the time, reset the timer and say, "You must stay here until the bell goes off. I'm sorry, but the time starts over." Make certain you follow through with the original directive even if you must miss other appointments.
- You need not stand right beside the child. But stay close so that you can keep your eyes and ears peeled for noncompliance.

A very effective tactic for dealing with chronic discipline problems is a form of ignoring. I call it "passive resistance."

- The passivity of this tactic is contained in this statement: I refuse to do what feels good to you if you continue to do what feels bad to me.
- Not fixing treats, refusing to run a "taxi service" and failing to take phone messages are mild forms of passive resistance.

- Not fixing meals, refusing to do laundry and giving no money are more severe forms.
- You can individualize this discipline by refusing to do the special things that your child likes. For example, not taking the child shopping with you.
- In order to avoid arguments and promote understanding, give your child a list of behaviors he or she has been engaged in that causes you to institute this tactic. Do this *before* you implement the passive resistance.
- Passive resistance should be used on problem behaviors that occur regularly, like failure to do chores. Make certain the misconduct is a long-standing problem.
- This tactic is especially effective for combating the chronic laziness or forgetfulness that develops in some preteens and teenagers.
- You can resume doing the things you quit doing at about the same rate that your child shapes up.

Work details permit children to work off their punishment just as the military gives KP to soldiers to motivate them to mend their ways.

- Work details can take many forms, *none* of which should be a part of normal everyday chores. Don't make the work too glamorous. In fact, a boring job should be considered.
- The best way to use work details is to assign a certain number of hours that must be completed before any privileges are enjoyed.
- Work details can be a consequence of violation of curfew or chronic laziness. For other ideas, see the chapter on Work and Chores.

Yelling and screaming are not usually good procedures. However, there is a way in which yelling can be effective.

- To be an effective punishment, yelling must be quick, loud and startle the child.
- The more often you yell, the quicker yelling loses its startling qualities. You should not yell more than once or twice a week. If you do, you run the risk of your kids ignoring you.
- Don't punish any further after yelling. If you truly startle the child, yelling should be sufficient.
- Remove yourself from the area after yelling. Return in about five minutes and carry on a normal conversation.
- If you use yelling as a startling technique, it's a good idea to explain yelling this way, "I yelled at you so that you'd wake up and see what you're doing. Next time, maybe you'll use your brain and see what you're doing without me yelling." Use the chart in the Appendix to reduce yelling.

Fining is an excellent form of punishment provided the child appreciates the value of money and doesn't like to lose it. Here are a few PRESCRIPTIONS *for the use of fining.*

- Fines should be paid within twenty-four hours of being assessed. If the child doesn't have the ready cash, then a work detail should be assigned by which the child can work off the fine.
- You may wish to double the fine for a second or third offense.

- If fines don't work relatively quickly, then your child probably isn't hurt all that much and money isn't as important as you first thought.
- In some instances, your fines will work best if you make yourself subject to the rule. For example, everyone, including Mom and Dad, has to pay a dime for leaving lights on when a room is not in use.
- Put the fine money in a special coin bank and, when it builds up to a few dollars, take the entire family out for a small treat. You'll find more hints in the chapter on Money.

Taking possessions away or denying privileges is a very powerful punishment. However, it is a little more complicated than you might imagine.

- If the privilege or possession isn't important to the child, then taking it away is more of a pointless insult than a punishment. Hence, make certain the child really values the privilege or possession. The best way to know this is to observe what the child enjoys and what he or she will work for as a reward.
- Another way to find out if the privilege or possession is important is to see if it creates the motivation to shape up when it is taken away. If the deprivation doesn't work within a day or two, then it isn't a very good penalty.
- For the first offense, set a short time period of denial. You can always increase the time for a second offense. However, if you find yourself constantly increasing the time, then you probably should switch to withdrawal of another privilege or possession.

There are many things you can do to control disruption that are just short of actual punishment. Here are just a few:

- IGNORING has many positive benefits. When you ignore, you simply remove your attention from the disruptive child. He or she doesn't get it back until *after* they have behaved properly for at least a few minutes. The only problem with ignoring is that you have to remain strong and not pay *any attention* to the child until he or she behaves himself/herself.
- ACTIVE IGNORING occurs when you purposely disregard a child's comments, even as he or she sits beside you.

  For example, your child is complaining about your being unfair, and, without acknowledging his or her complaint, you ask a question completely unrelated to the complaint, such as, "How was school today?" This gentle movement away from complaints works best with younger children.
- REMOVAL can be a sanity saver in that you simply tell a disrupter to leave the area. If you're about to blow your cool, you can always *remove yourself.* This gives everyone a chance to calm down and get a fresh start on the problem.
- STOPPING certain behaviors is often another way to avoid a vicious circle. When a child (or a parent for that matter) is caught up in an irrational argument or senseless emotions, calling STOP! can be the first step to making things work better.

Some good punishments are rendered useless by simple

oversights. See if these things are hurting your authority.

- TOO MUCH MATERIALISM helps children think that the "good life" is their due and doesn't have to be earned and protected. If your kids have too many toys or easy access to "goodies" and you deny or take them away, the kids will feel that you are denying them a fundamental right of being alive. Make sure your children *earn* what they get.
- TOO MUCH TALKING about the whys and wherefores of your punishment can give children the idea that you're not really confident in what you're doing. It also tempts them to try to talk their way out of the punishment. Once your kids know they've misbehaved and you know that they know they have punishment coming, simply do it and get it over with. Stringing out a punishment with too much talking is very close to cruel and unusual treatment.
- MISPLACED ANGER can cause your punishment to die on the vine. It usually happens this way: The child is a chronic disrupter and Mom pulls her hair out trying to find a way to make the child shape up. Finally, in exasperation, Mom blows her top, yells and screams in anger and immediately punishes the child. The child gets the notion that, "I got punished because Mom got mad." This leads the child in a fruitless search for a way to keep Mom from getting mad. Since the child can't control Mom's emotons, he or she never finds the key.

  All the while, the child misses the point. If Mom were to delay the punishment until after she got over her anger, the child would get this message: I got punished because I didn't do what I was told to do. With this lesson, it is just a short jump to this piece of logic, If I want to avoid the punishment in the future, I should do as I'm told. *Hence the timing of anger and punishment becomes terribly important and easily overlooked.*

- GUILT VS. REGRET. Many punishments fail because kids feel *guilty* instead of feeling *regret*. Guilt provokes internal uproar and self-condemnation while regret stimulates constructive change. You can avoid this pitfall by consistently rewarding positive behavior and punishing negative actions. Furthermore, don't keep reminding a child of a past mistake. A proper punishment is sufficient. If you continue to rub the child's nose in past errors, you will stimulate new guilt and/or rebellion.

- OVEREXTENDING A PUNISHMENT can cause an otherwise effective penalty to lose its disciplinary qualities. The best way to avoid this oversight is to observe the following rule about punishments: The quicker a punishment is over, the better. If a punishment drags on too long, the child becomes accustomed to the pain or inconvenience and the penalty ceases to be a punishment.

In some ways, rewards are more important than punishments. You can't teach right from wrong by always focusing on the wrong. In fact, focusing on the "right" makes your punishments much more effective, and you end up punishing less as you enjoy your children more.

- Good rewards often include the opposite of

the punishments discussed above. That is, you extend a curfew, suspend certain household chores for an evening, give a couple of dollars as incentive and arrange for special outings with Mom or Dad.

- Your rewards should outnumber your punishments in a two-to-one ratio. Thus, for every harsh word you say to your kids, you say two kind words.
- Don't forget that many kids respond to positive attention as the best reward of all.

SPECIFIC CONCERNS
Alphabetized for quick reference

Baby-sitters and Day Care

When both parents are working, reliable baby-sitters or day-care workers are worth their weight in gold. These substitute parents have a great influence on your children. But you need not feel guilty for having such helpers. Just make certain that they provide love, guidance and a positive environment for your kids.

I won't try to convince you to use baby-sitters or day care; that's a decision for you to make based on financial concerns and locale. I do ask you to consider my PRESCRIPTIONS for baby-sitters and then apply these plus a few more if you select a day-care alternative.

The baby-sitter should be an extension of you.

- The baby-sitter should share your fundamental values about the quality of life and the need for responsible and rational discipline.
- The sitter should have a reputation for excel-

lent physical and emotional care of children. Talk to your friends or ask a potential sitter for references.

- If you're new in town, go to a Newcomer's Club meeting and ask about sitters. Or go to your church/temple and seek information about child care.
- To evaluate a potential sitter, contact the licensing division of your local child care agency and apply state guidelines to a sitter.
- If the sitter has a problem with your child but you believe that the sitter does a good overall job, help the sitter learn how to solve the problem rather than immediately stepping into the middle of the situation. The child must learn to adapt to new authority figures.
- During your initial interviews/discussions with a sitter, keep your eyes and ears peeled for a jolly sense of humor. Being young at heart is a key ingredient in a successful sitter. Sitters who know how to play with children will have much more success in dealing with problems.
- Stop by the sitter's house once a month and just talk about your child/children. Exchange views about handling situations. Keep your pride in check, the sitter may be able to teach you a thing or two about your child.

If you elect day care, use the above hints plus a few more.

- Make certain the day-care center is licensed by the state and/or local government. This will ensure that proper care is given.

- I suggest you expect more structured activity. You may want your children to be exposed to some enriching experiences such as reading, writing and drawing.
- Be willing to expose your children to many different types of kids. They will eventually have to learn how to get along with all sorts of people.
- The older your child, the more you might want to place him or her in a day-care center that would offer some elementary preparations for formal schooling.

Back Talk

Most parents hit the ceiling when children engage in back talk. "You can't make me," "Taking out the garbage is dumb," and "Why can't my chores wait?" are just a few of the things that parents believe their kids must never say.

I think it's unrealistic to expect that your kids must never talk back to you. There's no question that back talk must be controlled but I don't think you can teach control if you get so upset that you lose control.

These hints will help you maintain a rational posture in this irritating situation.

- Make a distinction between back talk and disrespect. Back talk occurs when kids complain about a job or directive. For example, these things are back talk: "I don't have to do it," or "I'll do it in a minute."

  Disrespect occurs when children say

something nasty about you rather than about what you asked them to do. These things are disrespectful: "You make me sick," and "You think you're a big shot."

- If you encounter back talk, your best strategy is to make certain that the job is done. If you don't talk back to back talk, the kid will give it up and simply do what you asked.
- If you encounter disrespect, you need to do something more. You may have to implement a penalty—grounding, no television or an extra chore. You should also review whether or not you are too harsh in your parenting and are thereby stimulating rebellion.
- If back talk comes from a younger child or appears to be a good-natured attempt to manipulate you, you can react with humor. Make a funny face or goofy sound in answering back talk. Or tell a funny joke in order to let the child know that you're not taking the back talk seriously.
- I have found that much back talk results from children expecting you *not* to follow through on your directives. Once kids know that you mean what you say, they won't bother with back talk simply because it won't get them out of the job. Rather than waste time talking back, they will do what you asked.
- If your children seem to be constantly talking back, think about increasing your Positive Family Activity (see earlier chapter). Your kids could be telling you that the family has become a negative place to be.

Bedtime, Mealtime and Curfew

Teaching children awareness of and respect for time can make life a lot easier for you. It also prepares the child for the demands of the real world. If your children have problems with procrastination or forgetfulness, don't get into lengthy explanations about why time is important. Remember, appointments and schedules are a product of the adult organization, and children will never truly understand why we have such limitations. By the way, sometimes I don't either, but we all still have to live with them.

You can use time to help your children develop self-control. One way is to teach your children to get themselves up in the morning.

- Beginning somewhere around age 9 or 10, if not before, expect your children to wake themselves up in the morning. Make certain the child has a reliable alarm clock.

- If, during the first few weeks, the child doesn't get moving soon enough, wind the alarm up and keep it ringing until the child gets moving.
- Resist the temptation to nag or give constant reminders. Let the ringing bell do the nagging.

Along with getting up by themselves, expect your kids to put themselves to bed.

- Children should be able to put themselves to bed at or near 4 or 5 years of age.
- Permit approximately a half-hour between bedtime and lights out.
- The younger the children, the more you might coax them to bed, e.g., you might say, "You can continue to play in your dreams."

When school is in session, children should prepare themselves adequately to be ready to leave when their ride (bus) leaves. If the child is slow or misses the bus, consider these hints.

- Put a slow-moving child to bed one hour earlier that night. This procedure applies to all ages.
- If the problem becomes chronic, you may elect to use first- or second-degree grounding (see chapter entitled "The Reward of Punishment"). Or you may drive them to school but not write an excuse and let the school's penalty for unexcused lateness, e.g., in-school detention, take over.

Younger children who refuse to stay in bed, or who disrupt the activities of other members of the family must be taught that lights out also means to remain quiet.

- If the child keeps wandering into the family room or keeps asking for something, give him or her a choice. Say, "Either you stay quietly in bed or you will stand in the corner [somewhere in the hallway] until you decide to go to bed." Of course, make sure you follow through with this threat.
- If the child wakes the baby, temporarily put the baby in another room away from the disruption and ignore the disruptive child. Or use standing in the corner as suggested above.

Curfew probably is the most important rule in your home. Children should be responsible for coming and going according to some rules, no matter what their age.

- Within limitations (see next section), curfew can be negotiated and exceptions can be freely granted.
- You can use a negotiated curfew to give children more room to exercise responsibility, provided they have a good curfew record.
- Once you set a curfew, do not change it unless it is renegotiated ahead of time or emergency circumstances necessitate change.
- If your child calls you from a friend's house or party and asks for a curfew extension, you can agree, provided that the child asks politely and is doing well in major areas of responsibility (grades, chores, money).

Setting curfew times can be a complicated business. Here are some examples of appropriate curfews.

- *Children ages 5–10:* Children should come home thirty minutes before dinner and you should know exactly where the child is at all times.

- *Children ages 11–14:* The child should check in when the sun goes down and the streetlights come on. You may wish to change this to take into account the late hours of summer daylight and early sunset of winter. The children should inform you of any change in their location.
- *Children ages 15–18:* A general rule of curfew would be as follows: 15-year-old, a 10:30 P.M. curfew; 16-year-old, 11 P.M.; 17-year-old, 11:30 P.M.; and midnight for an 18-year-old. During the school year or when the kid has to work the next day, these curfews apply to *weekends only.*
- *For high school juniors and seniors,* you may be willing to negotiate a curfew up to 1 A.M. Curfews later than 1 A.M. should be very rare, negotiated for special outings (prom).
- *Kids ages 19 and older* (college age) who still live at home or who spend summers at home must agree with you on some type of curfew. Your negotiations with these kids can be very informal.
- Weekday curfews during the school term should be conservative. My PRESCRIPTION is that going out on a school night requires that the child has a specific purpose, even if that means just going to a friend's house to study. Likewise, the curfew for all children on school nights should be no later than 10 P.M.
- All children should be expected to spend at least one night at home. No outside activities are permitted that evening unless they are very special and negotiated ahead of time.

Arguing about being late can become a headache. Avoid the hassle with this PRESCRIPTION.

- Designate an official clock, either one in your bedroom or in the hall. If that clock says the child is late, then the child is late.

If older kids wish to stay up late (midnight), consider these hints before automatically saying No.

- Children should always be encouraged to get eight hours of sleep.
- If children are able to stay up late and still get up and get their chores done by a reasonable hour, don't bother them.
- Obviously, you permit later hours on weekends or when there isn't a demanding schedule the next day. Everybody needs to sleep in late sometimes.
- If the kids show any sign of irresponsibility due to the lack of sleep, enforce a bedtime for one week and then give them another chance.

Kids who are chronically late for appointments should be given a lesson in natural consequences. You can help it along by reminding them what it feels like to be disregarded.

- Apply passive resistance by failing to run errands for them or not taking them to important functions (see earlier chapter, The Reward of Punishment).

Mealtime should be a time of family togetherness and joy. Use these hints to make things go smoother.

- If a child continues disruption after one warning (preferably in the nonverbal form of a disapproving look or a snapping of fingers), simply take the food away and send the child to his or her room. Make sure there is no sneaking of food or other eating until the next meal. After dinner, explain to the child that you cannot tolerate disruption during meals and that you hope he or she will remember that next time food is served.
- If the child is late to a meal, you have two choices. If the problem is chronic, you can remove the food when the rest of the family is finished, even if the child isn't. If the disruption is rare, pemit the child to finish but he or she has to clean up.
- Follow the dietary guidelines contained in Dr. Lendon Smith's *Foods for Healthy Kids*, McGraw-Hill, 1981.

Car

I love to see a kid get a driver's license, provided that his or her parents supervise the use of the car *very closely*. If a teenager knows that Mom and Dad are watching, he or she will have greater respect and fear for a dangerous piece of machinery.

Tight control on the availability of the car gives parents the opportunity to teach children a lesson in maturity that they can use for the rest of their lives. The lesson is so simple that most of us have forgotten that someone taught it to us. That is, YOU PROTECT YOUR RIGHTS WITH RESPONSIBLE CONDUCT.

There are many variables to consider when making a car available to a teenager. Here are a few that should meet with common agreement.

- Kids must have met state requirements for attaining and maintaining a license.
- Kids must contribute to the expenses of driv-

ing the car with money that they have earned.
- Kids must work to take care of the car, especially keeping it clean.
- Kids must drive according to the guidelines you set down.
- Kids must be willing to run errands for you as part of their driving responsibilities.

To permit a child to own a car is a difficult decision. There are arguments to be made on both sides. Whatever your bias, here are a few PRESCRIPTIONS *to guide your thoughts.*

- Don't buy a new car for your child as soon as he or she gets a license.
- If you let your kid buy a used car, make certain that he or she has a substantial down payment and enough cash flow to support the monthly payments without getting behind.
- If you advance some of the down payment, make certain that you receive some kind of repayment, even if it's $10 a month for a year.
- If circumstances demand that a kid have a car at his or her continual call, make certain that the kid earns money to pay for car expenses.
- In most cases, I advise that the kid must be able to pay at least the added insurance payment that results from his or her being a teenage driver.
- Be very willing to negotiate a special deal if the teenager has better-than-average grades. Even the insurance companies agree with this deal.

Generally speaking, I don't believe that kids should drive to school. However, I can see some exceptions to this opinion.

- Children will be expected to take the school bus unless you give special permission for a specific occasion.
- You may agree to allow some driving to school so that your child may engage in after-school activities. *This is done as a convenience to you.*
- If you decide to give permission for your kid to drive to school, restrict the privilege to once a week for students who maintain above-average grades.

You can avoid hassles by assigning driving privileges by miles per week. Questions and arguments about taking the car are practically eliminated.

- Limit car mileage to a specific number of "pleasure miles" per week. You set the number of miles by discussing with the teenager the typical weekly activities and then making adjustments in the first couple of weeks. I've found that starting with 40 or 50 miles a week is fairly close to what you'll eventually end up with. This number will be adjusted depending upon how far you live from the kid's "pleasure centers."
- Pleasure miles accumulate as the kid drives on non-duty-related outings.
- Be willing to negotiate about driving to and from extracurricular activities. The guiding rule is deciding how much you want the child to participate in a particular activity.
- Pleasure miles not used one week can be

carried over into the next week only. Every two weeks, you should start fresh with the agreed-to number of miles. Kids may borrow up to one half of the next week's miles *provided* that they have had no infractions of car use for the past month.

- Someone in authority must check the odometer reading to corroborate the daily log *maintained by the kid.*
- Driving to school is to be considered pleasure miles if bus service is available.

If you don't like the pleasure miles concept, consider assigning so many hours per week.

- Activity by the hour should follow the same general rules as the pleasure-miles procedure.
- When the car sits somewhere for several hours (at the bowling alley, skating rink or school parking lot), those hours count against the total.
- A running log of hours of use must be maintained by the teenager and checked regularly by someone in charge.

See that the teenager shows respect for the car by keeping it clean.

- The teenage driver should clean the car, inside and out, on a regular basis without being reminded.
- If the car gets dirty, don't keep nagging the kid to clean it. Simply deduct a few miles or an hour or two from the weekly allotment as a way of saying, "Keep the car clean."
- If the problem becomes chronic, you may choose to repossess the car for a week.

Getting the car home late should be dealt with separately from any possible curfew violation. In fact, being late with the car is much worse than simply being late.

- Deduct a certain number of pleasure miles or hours for being late with the car. Increase this number if the problem persists.
- If the infraction is a minor one, you might deduct the miles or hours but still permit the kid to ride with someone else.

If your kid gets a speeding ticket, keep your head. It doesn't have to be a terrible thing.

- Resist the temptation to yell, scream and lecture. It doesn't necessarily indicate that the kid is a bad driver. He or she could have made an honest mistake.
- However, the mistake must result in a penalty. The teenager should have to pay the ticket from money that he or she earned.
- You may deduct some miles or hours of driving if the teenager has had a questionable record up until that time. Otherwise, let society teach the lesson.
- The kid had certainly better show some regret over the ticket. Keep your ears peeled for any bragging. If your kid brags about the ticket instead of showing some type of fear of future tickets, you might decide to deduct a few miles or hours.

If your kid comes home with the car and you get any indication of alcohol or marijuana consumption, implement a very severe punishment.

- Depending upon the severity of the offense, you should implement a fifth-degree grounding (confined to room) for at least two days and possibly up to ten days.

- During the grounding the kid is allowed to have no friends in, no phone calls, no snacks, no television or music, and may even have to eat all meals in his or her room.
- After the grounding is over, place the kid on two to four weeks "probation," during which you cut pleasure miles in half, occasionally follow the child while he or she is out with the car, forbid anyone from riding with him or her and keep your eye out for anything suspicious, like beer can tabs in the car, bittersweet smell of marijuana or the ashes from home-rolled marijuana cigarettes.
- Make certain the kid gets the message, "I will not tolerate any indication that you are flirting with death by driving and drinking or smoking marijuana."

Cleanliness and Orderliness

Children need you to set and enforce no-nonsense standards of personal cleanliness and daily orderliness. These habits will last the child a lifetime, not to mention giving you some relief from constantly reminding the child to "Wash your hands," "Brush your teeth," "Pick up your toys." A little effort in the beginning will save you time and energy later on.

Each parent has a different definition of clean. However, I don't think you'll disagree with these ideas of clean.

- Active children will take a bath or shower every day.
- Children will brush their teeth every morning and night.
- Children will wash their hands and faces before coming to the table to eat.
- Children will comb, brush or otherwise

groom their hair before leaving the house for a formal function (school, piano lesson).

Active, healthy kids often forget to wash before coming to the table to eat. If this happens regularly, try this procedure.

- Look at the child with a knowing smile and say, "Go look in the mirror."
- For the teenager, simply say, "Don't come back until you've washed."

When determining what is "clean" and what is not, you must depend upon your standards. You had also better hope that somebody taught you how to be clean.

- Avoid the extreme of the "white-glove" inspection. Give your home that "lived-in" look.
- Demonstrate your standards of cleanliness to your young children by having them help you with your household chores. Take extra time and let them practice getting something clean.
- In case they try to pretend not to know, you can be assured that, by age 7 or 8, your children know what you expect when you say, "Clean your room."

Older kids can dump their rebellion on you by arguing about How clean is clean? Stick to your standards and don't argue.

- If they persist in arguing, show them what clean is by having them do all the household chores, under your supervision, for a week. If you have a cleaning lady, make the child follow the lady around and watch her clean.

For some reason or another, children the world over seem to forget to brush their teeth. Try this PRESCRIPTION *if one of those kids lives at your house.*

- Warn the child once that the next time you find evidence that he or she didn't brush his or her teeth, his or her bedtime will be fifteen minutes earlier than usual.
- Next time the child forgets, take this action without further warning, even if you must interrupt the child's favorite television show.

Tracking in mud can be a regular occurrence with an active child. Here's one way to handle it.

- Have the child get down on his or her hands and knees and clean up the entire hallway. If the problem becomes chronic, you could have the child perform the clean-up job during his or her free time.

Leaving a mess in the television-viewing room is another pain in the back. Take action before it gets out of hand.

- Turn off the television set immediately upon finding the mess. Instead of reminding the kids of the reason, just stand there and look around and say, "You tell me why I turned it off."
- If you catch the mess after they've finished watching TV, call them to the room, even if they're outside, and have them clean up the

mess and give them another small chore in addition.

- If you can't find the kids, or you don't have the patience to deal with them, clean it up yourself and then give them a work detail to compensate for your cleaning up after them (see the work-detail section of the chapter, The Reward of Punishment).

You can take a very simple action that teaches children not to leave the water running.

- Get a large jug, for example an old milk carton, and the next time the child takes a bath have him or her carry several gallons of water to the tub from a faucet outside or in the basement.

When you find toys, games, or sporting equipment all over the house, teach a lesson that you should only have to do once.

- Pick up the mess and put it in a trash bag. Put the bag in the back of your closet. Next time the child wants the items, tell him or her where they are and that he or she can't have them for a week. If a child absolutely must use one of the confiscated items, he or she can be assigned a work detail (clean some pots and pans) in order to compensate for the mess.

Clothes

Teaching children to take proper care of their clothes is an important part of developing responsibility. Children who look neat and clean on the outside will have a better chance of feeling neat and clean on the inside. My many years of experience with kids has taught me this lesson: If a child looks in the mirror and sees an animal, don't be surprised if he or she acts like one.

While I support parental standards that have much leeway about clothes, consider following these general rules.

- Enforce a dress code that enables children to dress like children. Don't permit children to appear older than they are. (More on a dress code below.)
- Once children start to school, involve them in the clothing budget that you must live with.

- All children will learn how the washer, dryer, iron and needle and thread work. These are survival tools that they will eventually need to be able to use.
- All children will have some responsibility, appropriate to their age and stage, to make certain their clothes are clean and put away neatly.

Follow this general rule when you are faced with kids who abuse their clothing.

- Obtain old but clean clothing (from family or Salvation Army or Goodwill Industries) and explain that you expect the child to respect his or her clothing or else the old clothing will be worn. If you go to this extreme, I doubt you'll have to follow through. But keep the old clothes handy for a week or two just in case the kid thinks you're bluffing.

When a child's clothes are left lying about the house, there are several different things you can do.

- Pick them up and put them in a bag and put them in your closet. When the child desperately wants the clothes, make the child clean them before wearing them.
- Or throw them all in the kid's closet and forget about them.
- Or don't permit the child to eat or watch TV until the clothes are picked up and put in their proper place.
- Or pick them up, put them away and fine the child an amount that equals the extent of the mess.
- Or, if the problem is chronic, have the child

pick up the mess *and* assign an hour or two of work details as a punishment.

Preteens and teenagers can create a big scene when they want clothes that are beyond their years. If you're faced with this hassle, try this.

- Check the chapter on Complaints, and find a response that you are content with. My suggestion is to say: "This is a situation in which your request is simply beyond my rules. If you can think of a more reasonable request, I might be willing to negotiate a rule that we can both live with."
- If the child is at all calm, explain the confines of your budget. Also explain that you believe that children should dress like children.

When kids want to spend their own money on clothing, keep an eye on certain things.

- If you question the child's budgeting ability, supervise the purchase to ensure quality and a fair price.
- Supervising a teenager's clothing purchases gives you an excellent opportunity to find out what's "in" in fashion as well as sensitizing you to any existing peer pressure on your child. This latter insight will help you help your child in other ways.
- I suggest that extravagant items be excluded from the wardrobe. For example, it is my belief that school-age children, no matter how rich or poor, should not be allowed to purchase extremely expensive designer clothes. (Sorry about that, Calvin.)

- However, if your teenager earns his or her own money and is typically responsible, you might decide to permit an extravagant purchase, provided the child uses his or her money to pay the *difference* between what you would have paid for a less expensive brand and the price of the extravagant brand. This kind of exception to a rule won't hurt when it is done on your terms.

As you know, I believe it is imperative that children be allowed to experience childhood. Therefore, keep your children dressed like children.

- Use your rational rules to impose a dress code on your children. Your standards of decency and propriety must set the guidelines.
- Here are a few suggestions: No panty hose for a 9-year-old. No bra for a girl who doesn't clearly need one. No tight-fitting jeans or sweaters, or shirts opened to the navel.
- The length of hair is less important than that it be well groomed.
- Accent "styled hair" and don't fight about the length. Don't permit dyeing of hair unless extremely unusual circumstances prevail.

If the children violate your dress code, don't look the other way.

- Don't permit a child to leave the house if he or she is dressed inappropriately.
- Refuse to launder clothes that violate your standards. Or, to get tougher, impound the clothing without arguments.

Complaints

When you set limits on children's growth space, they will be unhappy about it. When kids want more, more, more, complaints will inevitably result.

In most homes, complaints begin and end with a mad mixture of do-nothing words. These words muddy the waters of action as they sharpen negative feelings. Parents get sidetracked from action when they respond to complaints with anger, guilt or some other useless emotion. As a result, complaints usually make matters worse.

Kids don't help the situation. Many of their messages are wrapped in hidden meanings, half-truths and exaggerations. When these things interact with parental uncertainties, complaints lead nowhere fast.

Complaints don't have to be so disastrous. They can serve a constructive purpose. They can clear the air, indicate emotional involvement and, best of all, give you a chance to discuss problems in such a way that constructive action follows. Complaints, if well managed, can be the first step toward implementing a policy where your word means something. You don't have to run for cover just because your children are raining on your authority.

To make children's complaints productive, try these strategies:

When a child has a difficult time achieving in school, you might hear, "If it weren't for the teacher, I would get good reports from school."

- You can respond, "You mean to tell me that you're not smart enough to figure out a way to get the teacher to like you?"
- Get the child to pinpoint several ways he or she can use positive public relations techniques on the teacher. Two good ones are to ask for help and say Thank you when receiving it.
- Keep your child's attention focused on his or her ability to take charge of the situation rather than be at the whim of classroom procedures.
- In general, lead the child to see how his or her misbehavior or failure to study creates a negative reaction in others. Then you might be able to say, "If it weren't for some of your behavior you wouldn't have the trouble you do."

Every parent who has made an unpopular decision has heard this complaint: "But, Mom, you're just not being fair."

- A response something like this works best, "I can see your point. In fact, you're right. Sometimes I must make decisions that you

don't like and it's natural that you will think I'm being unfair."
- Continue the conversation in the direction of discussing how life isn't fair and how the child must learn to tolerate certain frustrations.
- Avoid getting caught up in attempts to be fair. Whenever possible, do your best to be *just* in your rewards and punishments. But "fair" is a blind alley that creates nothing but negative feelings.

Peer pressure comes into full bloom sometime during the preteen years. That's when you'll likely hear, "But everybody gets to do it."

- There's an important message in this response; "You won't be treated like 'everybody.' You should know that by now. I won't be your parent and then turn around and treat you like you're just another member of some herd."
- Follow this comment by explaining the importance of individual morality. Also get some further ideas by looking at the PRE-SCRIPTIONS contained in the chapter on Peer Pressure.
- You can add a little humor to the situation by reminding the child of the last time that he or she demanded to be treated as an individual, a contradiction that causes you to turn gray.

Children can blackmail parents without ever realizing what they are doing. Be careful of the blackmail expressed in this complaint: "If you loved me, you'd let me have the things I want."

- A gentle, but firm confrontation works well in this situation. "*If* my eye! I do love you and you know it. I'm doing my best to help you grow up in a tough world. Why don't you try to help me a little?"
- This complaint is one of those that is so groundless that any further discussion should *not* center on whether or not you love your child.

This complaint can cause you to take stock of your parenting style. "You're always acting like a big-chief parent. You just love to put me down."

- Once you're sure that you express your love unconditionally and give the child ample rewards and recognition, you might reply, "If you remembered to live by the rules, I wouldn't have to use my authority. So if you want me to stop parenting you, see if you can parent yourself more often."
- Explain to younger children that they must learn to use their brains in exercising more self-control. You might say, "If you train your brain, then your brain will help you stay out of trouble."

Here's a complaint that is sure to get most parents off balance. "You just don't understand me."

- I know you're tempted to say, "I understand you more than you think." But this just leads to arguments. Instead try this response, "You're right, I don't understand you. Explain what you see in this girl (why you enjoy this activity) and maybe I won't worry so much."
- With just a little effort, you can help your

child see that understanding is never a complete thing, but with mutual cooperation, it can grow.

It's easy to get trapped by this complaint. "Why can't you treat me like an adult?"

- Once again, resist the natural response, "I do, honey." Rather, give the child an important lesson in reality. "You're not an adult yet, honey. You do some things like an adult [mention one or two] but you still have some growing up to do."
- You can follow this response up with sharing information about parent-child roles and explaining that it's tough to be a responsible authority figure.

If you can get over the anger connected with this complaint, you can learn a valuable lesson. "I know what you're going to say, so spare me the lecture."

- After you check your anger, reply, "Hey, I've got a right *and* a responsibility to make certain you know what I think."
- Before getting too upset, consider whether or not you really *need* to lecture so much. Maybe the kid is right. Maybe your lecture is a repeat performance. If your child is at all mature, he or she knows what's right and wrong. There's no need to repeat the same old admonitions. Your child might quit listening to you altogether.

Here's a complaint that grows out of our materialistic society. "I never get what I want."

- This quickie complaint can mushroom into a

95

full-scale battle in a matter of seconds. Defuse any arguments with this response: "Many times you don't get what you want. That is true. For instance, you're not going to get what you want this time."

- Sticking to your guns without belittling the child will help reduce any peer pressure that might be operating on him or her.

Death

When children face death, their own or that of a loved one, they need considerable patience and understanding. They most likely will not comprehend what is happening and will have questions that can't be answered and thoughts that might not make much sense. Yet their lack of maturity is a blessing in disguise. While it prohibits them from understanding death, it gives them the resiliency to cope with it (maybe even better than adults can).

In order to provide a steady hand to children during a crisis involving death, I advise parents to seek support and guidance from a trusted confidant. Not only must parents find the inner strength to help the child, they must also find an outlet for their own grief and pain.

My PRESCRIPTIONS are woefully incomplete. I urge you to read the works of Elizabeth Kübler-Ross, a professional woman and a beautiful human being who understands more than she ever commits to paper but whose writings give any reader the strength to carry on with life.

As you work through the death experience, rely upon your love and compassion.

- Listening to the child becomes all important. Encourage the child to talk about death in any way that he or she chooses.
- Be slow to give interpretations or judgments. Many adults give lectures about Heaven and "God's will" as a way of cutting off discussion. When you do give your interpretation, *be honest* and be brief.
- Use questions such as, "What do you think?" "How can I help?" and "How does it feel?" to stimulate the child's self-expression. Be sure to let the child know that *any* expression, including anger, is okay.
- Resist the temptation to burden the child with your pain. You might say, "I feel bad too," but don't engage in endless catharsis.
- Without excessive confrontation, try to keep life going in, as much as possible, a normal fashion. This includes maintaining consistent discipline. If you suspend rules, you give the child the idea that death somehow excludes the rest of us from life.
- Dr. Kübler-Ross gives a poignant explanation of death suitable for children under the age of 10 in her book *Living with Death and Dying* (Macmillan Publishing, 1981). She noted that the human body is just a shell, as the cocoon is a shell, or house, for a butterfly. And butterflies are much more beautiful when they are free. When they leave the cocoon, they fly away. We do not see them,

98

but they begin to enjoy the flowers and sunshine.

I won't even attempt to improve upon such a powerful image.

Disruptive Teenagers

Disruptive teenagers can tear a home to shreds. Foul language, dangerous threats, chronic laziness, assorted illegalities, gross misconduct and general disregard for authority can rip the patience out of the most tolerant parent.

Teenage disruption comes in all shapes and sizes. There's the younger teenager who has lousy manners, stretches all the rules, underachieves in school and pushes everybody to their limits with unbelievable manipulations. There's the older teenager who doesn't come home on time, abuses drugs, becomes verbally (and sometimes physically) combative at the drop of a hat and shows total disrespect for the family. Then there's the majority of teenagers, who don't go to wild extremes with disruption, but do find ways to at least temporarily test their parents' sanity.

Parents of disruptive teenagers are typically exasperated beyond all rationality. They still love their child, but sometimes can't stand to be around him/her. These parents recognize that their child has problems, but when countless efforts to help prove futile, many turn their backs and wait for the child to "grow out of the stage," hoping that they can survive the nightmare.

I've found that helping disruptive teenagers is the most difficult challenge to any parent or counselor. But they *do* want help; they just don't want to admit it. They are sad, hurt, frightened and lack self-confidence. Yet, rather than openly deal with these things, they cover their insecurities with a thick shell of nastiness and disrespect. They are "sad smart alecks." They want help but they make it darn near impossible for anyone to get close enough to help them.

I've developed special recommendations for parents of disruptive teenagers. I'll offer them to you in seven steps. These recommendations have worked more often than not, but they are not infallible. However, even if the entire situation blows up in your face, you'll know that you gave your child the "best shot" of help and guidance that you possibly could. That way you won't be faced with the painful day when so many parents say, "If only I had . . ."

For what it's worth—I've found that most disruptive teenagers who fail to take advantage of their parents' guidance, return several years later and say, "Thanks for giving me your best shot. I'm sorry I didn't listen. I just had to learn the hard way. Thanks for loving me enough to do everything you could. You were right."

These helpful hints come with a warning: Getting to the bottom of teenage disruption may be hazardous to your marriage.

- Two bad habits can develop in the best of marriages: taking each other for granted and not being honest about personal feelings. Teenagers will discover these things quickly.

This can lead to kids unwittingly getting what they want by using one parent against the other.

- If you seek help for your family, be ready to take a hard look at your marriage. The sooner you clear up any possible marital problems, the quicker you'll be able to help the teenager.

Many of the dos and don'ts contained in this book are especially applicable to disruptive teenagers. Here are the don'ts in dealing with teenagers.

DON'T:

1. Argue, nag, lecture, preach or keep talking after you've made your point.
2. Talk back to back talk (see the chapter entitled "Back Talk").
3. Explain your position in the middle of negative emotions.
4. Be friendly, gushy or too sweet when confronted with hostility.
5. Hold up other kids as examples. Your values are the standard.
6. Hit.
7. Belittle or call the kid names.
8. Draw peers, relatives or siblings into a hassle.
9. Scream and yell constantly.
10. Threaten to do something you're not going to do.

It's easy to turn a blind eye to disruptive teenagers or go to the opposite extreme of throwing up your hands and kicking them out of the house. Follow these steps and then you'll know that you tried everything humanly possible.

103

Step one.

- Add up the child's level of responsibility, jot down specific examples of disruption and present your findings to the child at the most peaceful time you can find.
- Here are some words you might use to structure your remarks: "You haven't been taking care of your responsibilities lately [give examples]. I really don't want to have to hassle with you, but I must do something about your disruption. If you don't improve in these things, I will have to put my nose into your business."

Step two.

- You take the second step in dealing with disruptive teenagers when you back up the threat made in Step One. You begin your follow-through with passive resistance, refusing to do favors.
- Examples of this passive resistance would be: not ironing the child's favorite jeans or blouse; not fixing snacks; saying No to special requests that you ordinarily honor.
- Here's how you might explain your actions: "As long as you continue to do unto me what hurts, I will refuse to do unto you what feels good." Some have called this the reverse application of the golden rule.

Step three.

- When disruption persists, you can take a more active posture by taking away the good things. Examples of this punishment include the removal of such sources of pleasure as the telephone, television, and stereo.

- If you take this step, be prepared for significantly more uproar. Remember the don'ts and say things like, "I told you I was going to have to do something about your disruption. If you want the goodies of life, you have to earn them with responsible behavior."

Step four.

- The distinction between Step Three and Step Four is the difference between taking away the good and giving the bad. Step Four calls for you to impose a punishment. Examples of this punishment are grounding and assigning work details.
- If you take this action after trying the first three steps, you can honestly say to your child, "I've tried to get your attention the easy way, but you have demonstrated that it won't work. I don't like this any more than you do. If you shape up, I will quit hassling you."

Step five.

- If the first four steps don't work, you should seek professional consultation before proceeding to Step Five. Your authority has badly eroded, and a thorough clinical study of your situation is in order.
- Step Five includes the exceptionally potent "Snoopervision." Be very careful when implementing this procedure.

  Snoopervision is implemented when the teenager has not responded to Steps One through Four and there is evidence of dangerous behavior (drug abuse, sexual promiscuity, fighting). You "snoopervise" by searching the child's room, listening in on private conversations, following the child around town, or calling his or her friends' houses. You do this *after* warning the child of exactly what you will do and why. (See chapter on Privacy.)

Step six.

- You are reaching the end of the line. Before giving up, try to find the child an alternative placement. See if Uncle Charley, Aunt Harriett, your brother or sister, or another responsible adult or agency will give the child a home and supervision. A complete change of living conditions may help get the kid back on the right road.
- Introduce the idea to the teenager this way, "Your constant disruption tells me that you don't want to live here. You will have to leave. If we agree on a placement, I will continue to support you. If that doesn't work, I will be forced to ask you to leave the house."
- Here are a few alternative placements I've helped arrange: through a local university, a 16-year-old joined an Outward Bound program (consult your local university or get the book, *Outward Bound, U.S.A.*, Joshua Miner, Morrow, 1981); another teenager moved to his cousin's farm; a parent's good friend took a teenage daughter into his home in a remote village.

Step seven.

- Contrary to what you might hear or read, kicking a child out of the house is almost impossible to do. To see it through emotionally, you must reach the point where you can say, "I've tried everything humanly possible. But I can no longer tolerate the disruption, nor can I sit idly by as my child shows complete disregard for my values." You'll need this firm resolve in executing Step Seven.

- The easiest way to kick a kid out is to simply say, "Move out." Set a time limit of three or four days. Don't repeat the order.
- If this doesn't work, sack or box up all the kid's possessions and set them in the garage. Say, "I told you to leave. So take your things and leave."
- If the kid still doesn't leave, change the locks and lock him (her) out. If he (she) breaks in, call the police and have the kid arrested. If you remain very firm in your resolve and communicate this clearly, you probably won't have to involve the cops.
- If your child is a minor (say, age 15 or 16), and you still need to take this step, consult the local child-welfare agency or a private attorney concerning your rights and responsibilities. If the kid is in his (her) twenties, move ahead with the eviction procedure without delay.

Once you've reached Steps Six and Seven, the kid may suddenly profess to have changed his (her) ways. Use these hints to implement a gradual reentry program.

- Give the child a place to sleep (perhaps the couch) for three days. The clothes and other possessions should remain boxed up during this trial period. If the kid stays grounded, does extra chores and remains very respectful during this time, you can proceed to phase two of the reentry program.

- Permit the child some limited freedom (until 8 P.M.), but do not permit the possessions to be completely unpacked.
- The third phase must include some type of educational/vocational program. The child must return to school, vocational training or get involved in some type of work/study activity. The child should still not unpack his (her) things at this point.
- Once the kid has adjusted to curfew, chores and educational/vocational duties, you can be more assured that things really have changed. Then you can permit the kid to unpack and completely rejoin the family. If you permit it any sooner, you encourage a "revolving door" possibility. It's tough enough going through the entire process once let alone doing it over and over again.

Divorce

Divorce is a very stressful time for all members of a family. Rather than advance my notions about why it occurs, I will give you my PRESCRIPTIONS for making the best out of a bad situation.

Whatever the nature of your divorce, please follow this rule: *Don't put the children in the middle of your problems.* If you feel that you've already made one mistake, don't make another.

In my view, putting a child between divorcing parents is a subtle but lethal form of emotional abuse.

As you consider a divorce, you should include protective measures for any children involved. These measures should be agreed to by both spouses.

- As part of your agreement on divorce proceedings and financial arrangements, agree with your spouse about how to talk with the children. Say, "Maybe we can't live together, but at least let's agree to minimize the problems for the kids."

- If the attorneys stimulate paranoia or encourage you to fight with your spouse, ask them to help you solve problems, not create them. An excellent book to help you confront attorneys on this or any other issue is *Winning with Your Lawyer*, by Burton Marks and Gerald Goldfarb, McGraw-Hill Paperbacks, 1980.

Talking to your children about a divorce is extremely difficult. Here are some hints (and words) that will make it easier.

- "Daddy and Mommy won't be living together anymore."
- "You did not cause the breakup. It has nothing to do with you."
- "You cannot get us back together, so don't try."
- "We both still love you and will try to help you as much as we can."
- Whatever words you use, help the children see reality, even though it's not very pretty and it hurts.
- Don't expect the kids to totally understand. Ask yourself, Do I really understand what's happening to me? Chance are that you don't.
- Permit the children to talk out their feelings without you or your spouse interpreting, judging or "answering" those feelings.

If you're uncertain whether or not to seek help for your children, consider these hints.

- Seek outside help if there is any indication that the kids are being put in the middle. Here are some statements that one or both parents might make to children that indicate they are being put in the middle: "I want you to tell me what your mother (father) is doing with his (her) boyfriend (girlfriend)." "I want you to love me more than your father (mother)." "I want you to forget about your father (mother)." "If your father gave us more money, you could have the dress you want."
- If a child is already having behavioral problems, a divorce might very well aggravate those problems.
- The critical age for children going through a divorce is approximately 5 to 15. Children younger than this usually don't have much idea what's going on and children older understand more than you'd ever believe.

It sounds empty, but try not to worry about the kids too much. It won't do any good.

- You're going through the divorce too. All things being equal, the divorce will probably be harder on you and your mate than on the children.
- Your children will bounce back rather quickly, probably within a few months. The key to their bouncing back is you getting *your* life in the best possible shape so that you are consistent, loving and peaceful. Research shows that if there are no continual problems the effects of a divorce on children will run its course within nine months to a year.
- The PRESCRIPTIONS in the chapter on Part-

time Parenting will help you handle some aspects of your newfound single life.

If your ex-spouse fails to visit the children very often, you'll have to say something. To help you out of this sticky situation, try these words.

- "Your father (mother) still loves you, but he (she) is having some problems right now. It's not your fault that he (she) doesn't visit."
- "It hurts to miss someone. But you're strong enough to manage."
- "I don't know why he (she) doesn't come, honey. Do you want me to ask him (her) for you?"
- Whatever words you decide to use, don't lie to the kids. For example, "Your father (mother) is very busy and will get here as soon as he (she) can." This can backfire on you in that the child may decide that Daddy's (Mommy's) work is more important than he or she is; this can lead to rebellion.

Be willing to talk with your ex about the children. But be careful.

- Stick with clear and concise behavioral reports of any trouble. For example, "Joey is crying every time I put him to bed. I suggest you ignore it." This approach helps you avoid getting into arguments about child rearing. It also reduces the chance of your children playing one parent against the other.
- If you talk to your ex about infrequent visitation, ask him (her) to see the children more often for their sake, not yours.

Custody fights are very painful for all involved. Follow these hints to minimize the pain.

- Try to keep the kids out of the lawyer's office. Don't subject them to the adversary process.
- If the children are young (under 11 or 12), you and your spouse, with professional help, must decide what is best for them.
- Keep the children in the same house, school, neighborhood and near their friends for as long as possible.
- Joint custody can be worked out *if* you and your spouse have some degree of humanity and decency in your communication. Don't be afraid to seek help in working through this difficult arrangement.
- Consider "divorce counseling" in order to promote the best atmosphere for the kids. The goal of such counseling should be to get your bad feelings/memories/thoughts under control so that they don't interfere with raising the children.

Drug Abuse

In case you haven't thought about it lately, there's an excellent chance that your child has tried or will experiment with drugs. Now before you protest, "Oh, he wouldn't smoke marijuana or take pills," let me remind you of two facts. First, you've probably been successful in raising an independent child who, in turn, will inevitably use his or her free will to test the limits you've set. Second, alcohol is a very dangerous drug and is readily available to kids of all ages.

A recent survey by the National Institute for Alcoholism, Drug Abuse and Mental Health reports that 60 percent of our teenagers have smoked marijuana at least once, while 92 percent have tried liquor. My fifteen years of experience with kids suggests that the numbers are slightly higher. It's shocking to look at your own kids and realize that there is a better than 90 percent chance that they will dump some type of drug into their precious bodies between now and graduation from high school.

When I realize that an epidemic of drug abuse threatens to swallow our children, my emotions run from awe and amazement that such a thing could occur, to outright fear and panic that parents, teachers and other responsible authority figures are doing so little about it.

The following PRESCRIPTIONS are dedicated to prevention of drug abuse. Even if you have one small child, you can be doing something *now* that will reduce the chances of your child being caught up in this vicious social disease.

My drug abuse prevention formula has ten parts. The first five parts are covered in greater detail in the first few chapters.

- *Children's responsibility.* See that your children rank in the upper levels of my Responsibility Index (page 17). If your child scores at or near 15, he or she will have good self-discipline.
- *Realistic fear.* Respect for your authority includes a realistic fear. This fear will help the kid protect himself or herself. Check the chapter on Developing Your Authority.
- *Individuating activities.* All children will have at least one activity that takes them away from the sameness of their peer group. The chapter on Peer Pressure will help you understand this rule.
- *Resisting peer pressure.* You are right to be concerned about how your children handle peer pressure. Your ultimate weapon is encouraging the regular use of free will and individual choice. Reread the chapters on Getting Off on the Right Foot, Developing Your Authority and Peer Pressure.
- *Nonnegotiable rules.* You must never permit your children to think that taking drugs is

116

okay. Recheck the chapter on Rules. It will help you discriminate between negotiable and nonnegotiable rules.

The other five parts of my drug abuse prevention formula may seem insignificant to some, but I assure you they're not.

Proper nutrition.

- Eating is fun but it's also serious business. Help your children understand how proper nutrition is essential to their bodies.
- Books by Dr. Lendon Smith will help you help your children. They are professionally sound yet easy to read.
- If teenagers are "junk-food addicts," it's little wonder that they might also throw assorted drugs into their bodies.

Overcoming boredom.

- Kids who have a sense of responsibility and self-discipline know how to overcome boredom. Pardon me if I reword an old adage: "An idle mind is a dope pusher's paradise."
- The habit of sticking to a task until it's finished is a great help in overcoming boredom. Once your child begins a boring job (doing the dishes, washing the windows, raking leaves), see that he or she finishes it before playing or moving on to something else.
- Resist the temptation to be your child's entertainment manager. You can give a child suggestions for what to do, but don't do it for him or her. You might say, "I know you're bored and that's a problem. Here are some

things you might do. [Give examples.] I'm sure you're smart enough to decide what to do."

Supervision.

- Be they age 2 or 12, let your children know that the first time they try something new you're watching.
- When your children first meet and play with new friends, I think you should know who the friends are and where they live.
- When your children first go to the park, stop by and check out the situation.
- When your children go to a new school, have a first date or drive a car for the first time, be there before they leave and when they come home. You may not receive first-hand information about what they did, but at least give them a clear signal that you're interested in what happened.
- If and/or when your child accuses you of not trusting him or her, you can say, "I trust you in many situations, but not this one. If you show me that you can handle this situation, then I will trust you!"

Knowledge about drugs.

- There is no substitute for parental knowledge of drugs, their availability and effects.
- Ask your local police/sheriff's department for drug information.
- Another good source of printed material is your local mental health association.
- The best source of information is "street workers." These young counselors usually work with a local agency and are often called "advocates" or "outreach workers." If

street workers have some common sense and good supervision, they can give you the "inside dope" on dope.

- If you have an immediate need, look up the phone number of your local youth agency, call them and ask for help. If you're still in the prevention stage, ask your PTA or church group to sponsor a presentation by one of these fabulous young people.

Self-control.

- You have a right to drink liquor, your children do not. If you abuse this privilege, your kids will follow suit.
- If you insist on having a cocktail hour every evening, you run the risk of teaching your children to have a different kind of cocktail hour when they are out with friends.
- If you or your spouse abuse alcohol (or any other drug) get some help *now*! If you're not sure what to do, call Alcoholics Anonymous; they will help.
- If it turns out to be "One of those days," and you really need some booze, consider drinking where there are no children.

Family Dynamics

When Mom, Dad and kids live together in the same house, things get complicated. The dynamics can be mind-boggling. But if you add aunts, uncles, cousins and grandparents, things can quickly get out of hand.

Except for rare situations, I have a lot of faith in the nuclear family—that is, parents and children comprising a self-contained unit. I think this family unit should be responsible for the care and raising of the children. I don't like interference in that process from outside sources, be it Uncle Charley or the omnipresent Uncle Sam. Thus, I believe that the involvement of members of the extended family unit in the private affairs of child rearing should be minimized.

The more the authority of the family unit can be centralized in one or two parents, the easier it is for children to learn how to relate to authority figures in a constructive manner. My hints in this chapter assume that parents, not relatives, are raising the children.

Spats between Mom and Dad are part of living. Be calm as you follow these hints in helping children adjust to normal disagreements.

- Tell your children that your fights are the same as when two friends occasionally disagree about things.
- While you don't have to make up in front of the children, let them see that things return to peacefulness as soon as possible.
- You need not explain to the children why you and your spouse have fights. The more you talk about it, the more the children will be confused.
- Remind the kids to stay out of your spats and not to take sides.
- Never bring your kids into your spats by forcing them to listen to your problems or making them choose sides.
- CAUTION: The more you fight, the more you run the risk of constant emotional upheaval creating tension in the home and eroding your authority.
- If fights persist or become *abnormal*, seek marriage counseling.
- Keep in mind this viewpoint: There is nothing better for children than a good marriage between their parents; nothing is worse than a bad one.

Grandparents don't like to have to raise your children (at least, most grandparents don't). They want to enjoy their grandchildren. Maintain an even keel with these hints.

- If physical location permits, don't over use or otherwise abuse grandparents as baby-sitters. If you need their help, ask them to help you pay for a baby-sitter.

- If you handle discipline problems without worry about what grandparents will say, you increase the chance that they will say nothing.
- If you don't want grandparents butting into your family's business think twice before telling them your troubles.
- If grandparents become meddlesome, explain your position this way. "You raised me (my mate) to be independent and have a mind of my (his/her) own, didn't you? Well, now I'm struggling to do the same for your grandchildren."
- The grandparents I've talked with love my old-fashioned approach. You might give them a copy of this book and tell them you are working with my advice.
- Don't be afraid to ask grandparents for constructive advice on how to handle a specific problem. They love the children but also have the benefit of viewing your children more objectively than you can.

If you and your mate disagree on disciplinary measures, follow this procedure.

- Each of you make a list of the main behavior problems with your children.
- Make a list of the areas in which you disagree.
- Use my helpful hints to find agreeable strategies in the areas of disagreement. Be willing to compromise with your mate on some issues just as he (she) should compromise with you on others.

Lying and Cheating

Nothing infuriates parents more than a child lying or cheating. Parents consider such deceptive practices to be an insult to their love for their children. Very few parents handle this situation well. Typically, accusations and belittling are sandwiched between demands to know Why? Instead of taking constructive action, most parents' first impulse is to get even.

Yet, if you think about it for a minute, why shouldn't children try to take the shortcut of a lie or cheat? We've all tried it at least once (c'mon, be honest). A lie or cheat doesn't make a child evil. And, provided it's not a chronic problem, you can keep your cool and teach the child that honesty and truth, at least within your family, are a key to a good reputation.

I advise you to do something about lying and cheating. While it usually isn't a serious problem, it can lead to a deterioration of self-confidence and respect for authority if kids get the notion that nothing is sacred.

When a child lies or cheats, keep your wits about you. It's not the end of the world.

- Resist hounding the child for a Why? Chances are you will hear, "I don't know," which will only heighten frustrations.
- No matter what else you do, at least calmly let the child know that you know about the deception and you disapprove.
- You won't like it, but your children will probably lie and cheat sometimes and you won't know it. So constantly playing the role of "Supersnoop" won't do you any good.

Many parents inadvertently stimulate lying or cheating by saying or doing things that contain a lie. Children figure that, if you lie, maybe they can get away with deception.

- Beware of disciplinary measures that sound logical and fair but actually contain a lie. For example, I recently heard a popular psychologist suggest this way of handling a young girl who regularly forgot to take the garbage out: "Next time she wants to be picked up after an outing, simply don't show up. When she asks you what happened, tell her 'I forgot.'" If you did this, you would actually be lying. You didn't forget, you were trying to teach her a lesson.
- If you ask the child, "Did you empty the garbage?" *after* seeing a full garbage can, you are pretending you didn't see reality. The child may then concoct his or her own version of reality.
- Many parents use this pretense believing that a child's confession will prevent irresponsibility. I doubt this.

Many lies are obvious prefabrications intended to astonish parents. If you hear an outlandish lie ("I wrestled a gorilla"), use "natural consequences" to get a message across.

- "You say you saw a dog roller skating?" Well, you'd better turn off the TV and study your spelling so you can write a story about such an unusual event."
- "You're only eight years old and you say you beat up on two high school bullies? We'd better give you extra chores so that you can use up some of that extra energy."

You can use limited freedom and words about trust to teach a child that lying and cheating are wrong.

- When younger children (under age 10) lie or cheat, prohibit them from playing with friends for an hour or two, reminding them that their lie or cheat causes you not to trust them for a little while.
- Older kids who definitely know where you stand on lying and cheating probably should suffer greater restriction of freedom to get the message of trust across.

  You can implement varying degrees of tight supervision by doing such things as: not permitting the 11-year-old to go to the store by himself, making the 13-year-old skip her regular visit to a friend's house for two days, cutting back the 16-year-old's curfew by an hour for two weeks, and deducting several pleasure miles or one hour from the 17-year-old's driving privileges.
- If kids complete the first part of a timed restriction with minimal complaints, you might decide to lift the restriction. I encour-

age you to use a time-off-for-good-behavior option.
- If kids lie or cheat twice in a short period of time, say a week, you may wish to reduce such things as television time, use of phone and visitation of friends to your house.
- Once the supervision or other penalty is over, *do not remind* the child about the lie or cheat.

An innovative method for reacting to lying and cheating is called "overcorrection." If you use it, follow the procedure exactly.

- Shortly after discovering the lie or cheat, sit with the child in a quiet area and ask, "What is the lie?" or "What did you do to cheat?" Follow this question by asking, "What is the truth?" or "What is the thing to do to be honest?"
- These two questions should be asked in a calm supportive manner. *This questioning must not be harsh, punitive or otherwise belittling to the child!*
- The procedure should be repeated approximately five times, or until you feel the repetition sinks into the child and "overcorrects" the situation.
- Interrupt any complaints or attempts to stop the procedure, focusing instead on repeating the questions and answers.
- This procedure can stimulate unhealthy guilt in children. Therefore, *don't do it* if you're angry.

Sometimes you're not sure whether or not your child lied or cheated. You don't have to catch every lie or cheat in order to teach the importance of honesty.

- Don't browbeat children into a confession.
- Don't stimulate a guilt trip by saying such things as, "If you lie to me, my heart breaks and I die inside."
- Be honest in the face of a possible lie. Simply tell the child, "I think you lied to me (cheated), but I don't know for certain. I will watch you very carefully in the next few days. If I catch you in a lie or cheat, I will double the penalty."
- If you receive a spontaneous confession of wrongdoing, I suggest you apply tight supervision in a milder form than suggested above. You tell the child, "You received a penalty for your lie (cheat) but I'm cutting it in half because you told me the truth. Better late than never."

If lying or cheating occurs regularly, you may need to look deeper.

- Chronic lying or cheating can reflect many problems. Here are just a few:
    1. The child may feel too much pressure from you to achieve. He or she lies or cheats in order *not* to disappoint you.
    2. Lying and cheating may be an outgrowth of a child never learning how to overcome failure. While taking the easy road may work temporarily, it ultimately erodes a child's self-confidence.
    3. You may be giving the child too much attention for lying and cheating, thereby encouraging him or her to play a verbal game of "cops and robbers."
    4. The deception of lying or cheating may be a symptom of some other problem. For example, I've seen kids who were

molested by a stepfather, uncle or other close friend or relative begin lying or cheating as a way of dealing with their fear.

- Lying or cheating reflects on your authority and can mean that your child has lost some respect for you.
- Chronic lying or cheating is one reason to seek professional help. With objective guidance, you can look for the hidden causes.

Manners

As part of the entire permissive scene, parents have allowed children's manners to slip badly. We all want our children to behave with good manners, but most of us don't take the time and energy to build good manners in our children. As a result, we have children running around showing little or no basic respect for the rights of other people.

My guidelines in this area are very old-fashioned and I encourage you to start right now to make certain that your children develop good manners. There's only one way to do it—PRACTICE, PRACTICE, PRACTICE.

Here are some general guidelines to follow in developing good manners in your children.

- Manners is one area in which you won't be successful unless you set a good example.
- Bad language is to be considered a part of bad manners.

- Lengthy explanations about the reason for good manners are not necessary. It is sufficient to say, "Good manners are respectful of others and, as my child, you will show respect for other people."

There are common pleasantries that children should learn to use regularly. Make sure that these six are in the child's vocabulary.

Please.

- Children should be expected to say Please when asking for something during mealtime, requesting something from a teacher or store clerk, ordering in a restaurant or asking for a favor.

Thank you.

- Thank you or Thanks should be said many times a day by even the youngest of children. When food is passed, when receiving a special request or help and after being granted a favor, are just a few of the times that a child should say Thank you.
- Thank you should also be said via a card or note after a child receives a gift. Take time to help your child construct an appropriate thank-you note.

You're welcome.

- You're welcome should always follow when someone else says Thanks.

Excuse me

- As a matter of routine, children should say

Excuse me when such things as burping, accidentally cutting in front of someone, or interrupting a conversation occur, and when apologizing for a display of bad manners.

I'm sorry.

- Saying I'm sorry doesn't have to be overly sweet or dramatic to be effective. I'm sorry is appropriate in such situations as expressing condolences to someone, apologizing for a mistake or a showing of extreme bad manners.

I'll help.

- I'll help should be heard when a neighbor has a problem, you need help with a major household task or a younger sibling has a difficult homework problem, to cite a few examples.

Here are some other examples of good manners that should be part of children's everyday behavior.

- Saying Hello when greeting your friends and Good-bye when leaving.
- Shaking hands when appropriate.
- Rising to greet people when they approach.
- Calling your adult friends by their appropriate titles: Mr., Dr., Mrs., etc.
- Demonstrating good table manners—proper use of utensils, eating without excessive noise, asking to be excused before leaving the table are especially applicable.

Showing respect is a difficult behavior to define. Here are a few examples.

- Expose children to the internal feelings of being blind—a blindfold would do the trick—or to another handicap by simulating the handicap. This procedure will teach respect for people with handicaps, which includes not staring at them.
- Holding the door for older people or volunteering at a nursing home (for a teenager) will teach respect for older people.
- Explaining to your kids that being different doesn't make others bad can do much to teach them respect for the poor, the disadvantaged and racial/religious minorities.

"Bad language" is best treated as poor manners. Teach your children that certain words are considered by the majority of people to be offensive and hence are disrespectful.

- No word is intrinsically "bad" or evil. But, children must recognize the reality that certain words will get them into trouble.
- Don't worry about where your children hear certain words. The words are everywhere and children *will* hear them.
- The best way to teach control of "bad" words is not to use them yourself.
- If you hear a "bad" word used in the privacy of your own home, you may choose to simply remind the child to be careful with that word.
- If the word is said within a sensitive situation (in front of strangers, friends, relatives or in public), immediate disciplinary action is required. The least you should do is to demand (and get) an immediate apology. Standing in the corner, sitting on a chair, one night's grounding or one day without phone

privileges may be needed, depending upon the child's age and the situation.

- "Bad language" is one of those cases in which reality is not always logical. The majority are offended by certain words, a fact that may not be logical, but is nonetheless true. Your children must learn to censor those words in order to take advantage of the opportunities those people control. Once they reach adulthood, they can choose whether or not to continue the censoring.

When children demonstrate bad manners, keep your voice calm and take action consistently.

- Stop all activity until the child produces a response consistent with proper manners.
- Make the child repeat the correct behavior until he or she gets it right.
- Correct children in front of others without hesitation.
- If kids resist your request for compliance, take tougher action. For example, ask a disruptive child to leave the table, refuse to give the child what he or she wants until mannerly behavior is forthcoming.

Money

Money is an important factor in today's living and children must learn how to earn, save and spend it wisely. Even when a child earns his or her own money, you still have a responsibility to see that he or she budgets it carefully. And, above all, don't confuse money with love. They are separate issues. Both are important and one does not make up for the absence of the other.

Any financial responsibility you give to your children will develop in phases. Your best bet is to start early.

- *Phase One.* Ages 0 to 5. Children get the idea that earning money is directly related to work.
- *Phase Two.* Ages 6 to 9. Children get a weekly allowance that is related to daily responsibilities.
- *Phase Three.* Ages 10 to 13. Children get a weekly allowance that is indirectly related to

daily responsibilities. They do chores because they live in your house, not because they get paid to do them.

- *Phase Four.* Ages 14 and above. Children get no allowance. They earn their money through work contracts with you or an outside job.

Let's look at each phase in more detail.

Phase One

- This phase begins when the child is old enough to say, "Gimme that."
- Children earn a small amount of money immediately after successfully completing a "job." "You will get a dime if you help me take the trash out and feed the dog."
- Give the child the money and ask him or her what it will be spent on. Encourage the child to hold onto the money for at least a day or two prior to spending it.
- The older the child, the more you should expect him or her to hold onto money for a longer period of time.
- If the child loses the money, express your regrets but do not replace it.

Phase Two.

- This phase begins somewhere around the child's fifth birthday. I pick this age because it usually coincides with the added responsibility of beginning some type of formal schooling. You could initiate the phase earlier if you wish.
- The child receives a conservative weekly allowance in direct relationship to his or her

performance on a daily responsibility checklist. Fifty cents to a dollar per week is about right.

- To study the ins and outs of the responsibility checklist, please consult my book, *Keeping Kids Out of Trouble*, Warner Books, 1979, page 153.
- The child should be expected to pay for minor pleasure expenditures out of this allowance.
- It is the child's responsibility to earn extra money for a special outing. You may advance the money provided you follow the recommendations listed under the section on Loans in this chapter.

Phase Three.

- This phase should begin on or near the child's tenth birthday. I like the idea of beginning it *on the birthday* in order to better communicate, "You're older now and I expect you to behave older."
- The weekly checklist is suspended provided that the child has proven that he or she doesn't need the constant monitoring.
- The child's weekly allowance is slightly increased.
- The child is expected to continue chores around the house.
- Failure to meet responsibilities can result in fines or deductions from the allowance.
- Toward the end of this phase, children should be encouraged to find a new source of money that *they earn all by themselves.* For more about this idea see the chapter on Work and Chores.

- Don't forget to explain in detail what Phase Four will be like.

Phase Four.

- This phase should begin on or near the child's fourteenth birthday. Clear and concise explanation of the guidelines is imperative. This phase should prepare the child to leave home.
- Chores continue as in Phase Three, as do general reviews of responsibility and imposition of financial penalties.
- All allowances are suspended.
- Children must earn all pleasure money by working either at a regular job, baby-sitting, paper route, working in the neighborhood, or making work contracts with you to do jobs that are over and beyond daily chores. Examples of these work contracts might be: washing and waxing the car, scrubbing and polishing the floors, washing windows, cleaning out the basement or garage, or other such tasks around the house.
- Pay the child at least one half the minimum wage for these work contracts.
- Keep a list of possible jobs available but don't take responsibility for making the child work. Let financial need do that.
- Give the child help in finding job opportunities around the area. For more information, see the chapter on Work and Chores.

Just because a child earns his or her own money doesn't mean that you give up supervising purchases. Make certain a sensible budget is being followed.

- Let the child know that purchases that

exceed a certain amount are subject to parental review. You might set that figure at $50.

- Be very careful to review purchases involving cars, stereos, expensive clothing or any other item that constitutes a sizeable investment.
- Encourage the child to have a personal checking account and make certain you review that account bimonthly. Know what your children are buying.

Many parents unintentionally teach children that loans don't have to be repaid. They do this by "lending" children money and not "collecting" it.

- If you call it a "loan," make certain it is repaid in some fashion.
- If your child wants extra money for a toy or treat, give the money only if the child has a good reputation for repayment.
- Establish a repayment plan when the loan is given. In most cases, the loan should be repaid within a week. It's up to the parent to remind the child about the loan.
- Loans can be worked off by giving the child small jobs to do; for example, cleaning out the inside of the car or vacuuming the family room might repay a loan of $2.
- If children accept your No when asking for a loan, you might change your mind fifteen or twenty minutes later, saying, "I'll advance you the money because you didn't hassle me when I said No."
- In the case of bigger loans to older children (helping with down payment on a car), set up a repayment plan similar to the bank's. If the kid becomes two months delinquent in his or

her account, temporarily repossess the item.
To reduce conflict, put your agreement into
writing.

*Many kids get themselves into a financial bind by failing
to collect money from a job (say, a paper route) or
spending collected money on treats. If your child exercises
poor judgment with someone else's money, follow
these hints:*

- If you lend the child the needed money,
  make certain you institute a repayment plan
  according to the guidelines listed above.
- Tell the child, "You got yourself into a bind
  and you must get yourself out. I will help you
  but it's mostly your problem. You must face
  the music."
- If facing the music might cost him or her the
  job, you can bail the child out, provided that
  you restrict the child's freedom until he or
  she has worked out of the hole.

Music

Around the age of 11 or 12, your child will begin to experience teenage excitement. Along with the rising interest in boys (girls), special friends, telephone calls and trying to figure out all the ways that you are wrong, kids discover music. Radios blast, stereos shake the walls and parents are pressured into giving permission to attend rock concerts.

Music occupies an important place in a teenager's life. I'm giving music a chapter of its own because you need to pay attention to how your children express themselves through music.

They say rock and roll is here to stay. That's fine, provided the music doesn't pollute the air.

- If necessary, invest in a decibel meter and hang it next to the kid's room. When the noise edges near the decibel level that is disruptive to the serenity of your home, take action.

- Remind the child about the noise and then warn the child once.
- If this doesn't work, take the record that is playing and put it away for two days.
- On second offense, unplug the record player for two days.
- For a third offense, repossess the record that is playing and give it to a charitable organization.

Your child won't like your "interference" in his or her "artistic expression." Here are a few words to use when explaining your actions.

- "Blaring music is disrespectful to this family, and you know I will not tolerate disrespect."
- "You gave me your record by not heeding my warning."
- "You may have bought your own stereo and records, but I will take action against you if you don't use your things according to my rules."

The words to many popular songs are sexually explicit. You may choose to exercise some control.

- In order to figure out the words to a song, you might have to listen to it continually for a week. Rather than go buggy with this approach, simply ask your child to tell you the words to any song you are worried about.
- If the words are sexually explicit, don't automatically censor the song. It's probably better in the long run if the child is given the

chance to discuss all the ramifications of the words. It's a perfect opportunity to talk about sex.

- If the words deeply offend your morality, make a simple, *rational* statement that the song is not to be played in your home. It's unnecessary and impractical to tell the child that he or she can never listen to the song.

There are some circumstances under which kids can be allowed to attend rock concerts.

- Unless the child demonstrates exceptional responsibility, there should be no unchaperoned rock concerts prior to age 15 or 16.
- Don't accuse your child of wanting to go to a rock concert in order to smoke dope or be promiscuous.
- Use rock concert attendance as an incentive to encourage your children to improve their responsibility. Permission to attend can be *earned* by responsible conduct rather than be granted after your being threatened with some type of blackmail.
- Be willing to negotiate a late curfew once a semester. Use school performance as the manner in which the child can "prepay" you for the extra privilege. "Bring me a note from your teacher that says you got a B on your test and I'll let you stay out until 2 A.M."
- Treat rock concerts as your child's expression of his or her musical preference. Don't permit your like or dislike of the type of music to enter into your decision. Keep your eyes and ears on responsibility.

Part-time Parenting

Part-time parents have it tough. They don't see the children very often and when they do, it's nearly impossible to establish a consistent routine. Discipline and order take a backseat to enjoying every minute. You don't want to have to be tough with your kids when they'll be gone before you know it. So it's very easy to fall into the trap of being a weekend entertainment manager.

It's also no surprise that part-time parents tend to ignore disruption that ordinarily would call for discipline. But you must not throw away your authority just because you're excited to see your kids. If you act as a responsible parent, even on a part-time basis, your children will learn to respect your authority.

Part-time parenting is a strain on everyone concerned. It is something that both parents and children must learn to live with. The following hints will help you balance the excitement of being with the kids with the necessity of remaining a disciplinarian.

Here are a few tips that will make part-time parenting easier on you and the children.

- Post your rules for each child in a conspicuous place (on the refrigerator).
- Be willing to remind the kids of the rules more often than you might if they lived with you full time.
- If you're constantly entertaining the kids, it gives them an unrealistic notion of what life is like at your house. It also creates turmoil in their lives when they return to the other parent. So don't do it.
- Spend more time with the kids than money.
- Be honest with the children about how you feel being their part-time parent.
- Redouble your efforts to take disciplinary action without constant verbal hassling, arguments or other time-consuming, ineffective procedures.
- Avoid any statements that might make the kids feel guilty that they live with the other parent. For example, "I just can't understand why you want to live with your father (mother)."

If you're a weekend stepparent, you face twice as many potential problems. Keep these Prescriptions *in mind.*

- Follow all the recommendations given in the chapter on Stepparenting.
- Don't defer disciplinary action to your spouse.
- Talk to your spouse about feelings of being an outsider if indeed you feel that way. Don't do it in front of the children.
- You will need a list of primary rules that you

and your spouse agree must not be broken. However, minor infractions (shoes and socks not put away) might be overlooked in the interest of promoting a positive atmosphere. In other words, don't harp at the children about every little thing.

If you live close to your children, here are a few things you can do to stay in touch with their lives.

- Know the children's teacher(s). Visit the school during educational week (at least).
- Keep up to date on their day-to-day activities, grades, projects, extracurricular activities, friends, misconduct and special outings they've had.
- Offer to take their friends with you on some outings.
- Be sure to attend special functions as often as possible. For example, concerts, athletic events, recitals, etc.

If you live far away from your child/children, it's very difficult to stay in close touch with their day-to-day life. But try these things.

- Write a diary of the significant events in your daily life and send it to your child/children every couple of weeks. Encourage your child/children to do likewise.
- If your budget can possibly afford it, call your kids once a week.
- Do everything in your power to attend a special function at least twice a year.
- Try to spend an extended period of time with the child/children during the summer.
- Remind them of your love regularly.

Conflicts between full-time and weekend children can develop. Use these hints to minimize the problem.

- Once during the weekend, do something as a family, even if it's only a window-shopping outing.
- Regularly remind the kids that they are related, if not by blood, then by love.
- Use role reversal (see the chapter on Sibling Rivalry) to teach the children what it would be like if their roles were reversed.
- Establish as many cooperative play situations as you can possibly think of.
- Use the other PRESCRIPTIONS contained in the chapter on Sibling Rivalry to deal with these conflicts.

Peer Pressure

Pressure for conformity is part of everyday life. Advertisements tell us that the key to acceptance is buying the "in" thing. Most people censor their words and actions for fear that other people won't like them. And suspiciousness about others' intentions is becoming a necessary survival instinct.

Adults have the resources to cope with these pressures. We can utilize our free will and choose to follow our own consciences. But our children don't have the ego strength, understanding and experience to counteract the blind pursuit of sameness.

Combating peer pressure requires that we help our children develop mental resources. The nurturance of individuality is a vital part of any resistance efforts. This nurturance occurs as you gently push kids into the development of individual talents, hobbies, etc., as you set a good example of moral behavior, as you make certain that your children follow the rules that you establish, and especially when you refuse to go along with a child's demands simply because "Everybody is doing it!"

You can't battle the stampede toward sameness unless you are an adult who behaves in a manner worthy of respect. Thus, ask yourself, Is my conduct responsible? Also ask yourself:

- Do I practice what I preach? You may not always know it, but your children are watching you. What are they seeing?
- Do I stay informed? Never before has so much material been available that helps parents learn about the world their children must learn to cope with. Is your information current?
- Is my word my bond? If you have developed a reputation for meaning what you say and saying what you mean, you've taken a giant step toward being respectable. How's your follow-through?
- Do I truly listen to my kids? Listening to childrens' successes and failures is tougher than you think. It requires you to clear your mind and concentrate on what the child is saying.
- Do I play with my kids? You don't have to spend lots of money in order to play with your kids. There's a piece of you that still can be a carefree child. Are you a stuffy grown-up?
- Do I need drugs to be happy? Alcohol is a dangerous drug and many parents think they can tell their kids not to smoke marijuana while they are sipping their third martini. Do you control your intake of booze?

This may surprise you but children usually get their first taste of peer pressure from their parents. You can reduce the impact that peer pressure has on your children's lives by reducing it in your own life.

- See if you are saying any of these things: "But, honey, we *have* to invite the Browns, they are friends with the Johnsons and we can't afford to offend them." Or "I don't like them either, darling, but don't forget, they belong to *the* club." Or "Don't wear that dress (suit); can you imagine what people will think?"
- When you set standards for your children, don't refer to what other people think. Refer to what you believe in.
- Avoid pressuring your child into compliance with harmless-sounding comparisons, e.g., "Don't act silly, everybody will laugh at you."
- Be openly critical of mass media's pressure for conformity.
- Never give in to your children because they clobber you with "Everybody is doing it." You can respond, "I don't care about 'everybody.' I care about sticking to what I believe in."
- Don't argue about who "everybody" is. That's a bottomless pit from which you can't escape.

Don't allow a man-made institution to use an otherwise loving God to pressure your children into compliance.

- If you choose to expose your children to spiritual values, encourage them to question, challenge, and incorporate the beliefs into their personal lives.
- Be extremely wary of the pressure that can

result from threatening children with damnation, and other fear tactics. It only sets them up for rebellion in the future.

- Be willing to discuss the moral of Sunday school stories and add your personal beliefs.
- If you want the kids to read the Bible, make certain that their free will has plenty of space to make choices in matters of faith.

Competition often becomes so frightening to kids that, rather than try and fail, they simply don't try at all. Redefine competition in a healthy way.

- Reduce the pressure to look good in the eyes of others by explaining competition this way: "*Never* compete with another person, no matter what you're doing. *Always* compete with what you did yesterday and what your sense of values makes you want to achieve tomorrow. Improve upon yourself, not what somebody else wants you to be. Be your own pacesetter."
- When your kids say, "But, you're pressuring me to be like you," you can explain that they have plenty of opportunity to develop their individuality. You should remind them that you must provide guidance as they search for who they want to be. If and when you hear this complaint, you ought to review your rules and see if you've allowed room for exceptions. If you haven't, change some of the rules and negotiate exceptions to others.

Nothing works against peer pressure like the development of individual talents.

- Make it a rule that your kids must engage in at least one extracurricular activity that demands individual effort. Group activities may occur after the child demonstrates that he or she has adjusted to this individual activity.
- Examples of this type of activity would be: chess club, swimming, tennis, junior achievement, dance, gymnastics, running, and hobbies that accentuate individual achievement.
- If a child wishes to drop an individual activity, he or she must successfully start a new one before being allowed to drop the old one.

Coping with your child's "bad companion" is difficult. Follow this procedure in minimizing the hassle.

- Identify the trait you most dislike in the child's companion. Such things as brags too much, lies and acts too old are typical traits that parents don't like in their child's companion.
- Talk with your child about the trait you object to. Say, "Why does your friend brag all the time?" Or "Your friend tries to act much older than he is."
- When your child actively defends his or her friend, you know there must be a reason. To find that reason, think of a weakness that is the *opposite* of the trait you don't like in the companion. For example, lacks self-confidence is the opposite of brags all the time, feels like a baby is the opposite of acts older than his age.
- You might conclude that your child is

155

attempting to compensate for a weakness by being attracted to the companion. The child might be thinking, Maybe my friend's bragging will rub off on me and I will gain self-confidence.

- If this "compensation theory" sounds plausible, you can help your child deal with the "bad companion" by focusing your efforts on improving his or her own weakness. You may decide to give the child more responsibility and rewards as a way of increasing self-confidence. Or you could conclude that permitting more freedom would give a child a sense of maturity. If you use this process, you can actually use the "bad companion" problem to help your child improve.

Privacy

Privacy is a two-sided issue. On the one hand, kids should have privacy. It gives them the opportunity to develop their personal lives. On the other, they should learn to protect their privacy so that they can continue to enjoy it. Many parents aren't sure how to maintain this delicate balance.

Children usually take their privacy for granted. How many times have parents heard, "You had no right to go into my room!"? Just once I would like a child to say, "Hey, Mom (Dad), thanks for giving me a room in which to enjoy my privacy." Alas, privacy is one of those things that you must handle without praise. Your kids won't understand how difficult your job is until they have a home of their own.

You have a responsibility to teach a child to protect his or her privacy. Slow and easy is the best method.

- Your children should understand the general rule about privacy. For example, "You have a right to privacy provided that you don't abuse it."

- The younger children protect their privacy by: keeping their rooms clean, turning the music down when you ask once and not fighting with siblings while enjoying their privacy.
- Teach your children to knock before opening a closed door. If you do this when entering their room, they will do likewise with you.
- If you clean your child's room (not very often, I hope) don't look through his or her things.
- If you decide to violate a child's privacy by snooping through his or her things, I suggest you make it part of an overall program of "snoopervision."

Snoopervision is a very powerful technique. Be careful to follow these hints when implementing willful violation of the child's privacy.

- Warn the child of your intentions at least a few days ahead of time. You might say, "If you don't turn yourself around in the following ways [specify the problem behaviors], then I will be forced to violate your privacy."
- If you must implement snoopervision, you probably should seek some help from a professional counselor.
- If you actually "snoopervise," consider the following: search the child's room on a random basis, search the child when he or she arrives home from an outing, listen in on phone calls, read any letters that come to the

child, call your friends and ask them to check on your child, drop in on the child when he or she is out and follow the child in a friend's car.

- Suspend snoopervision as soon as the child proves that he or she is no longer extremely disruptive. In any case, *do not snoopervise longer than two weeks.*
- Use snoopervision *only* if the kid is showing no respect for your rules and you've tried all other forms of discipline first.

Public Disruption

Children who misbehave in public are not only violating your rules and regulations, they are also a source of embarrassment. Too often, parents are intimidated by their children's public disruption. As a result, children are not disciplined appropriately and usually learn that public disruption is an excellent way to blackmail parents into submission to their will. I believe that you should love your children enough to give them this message: "I will discipline you the way I always do no matter who is watching." After all, your children deserve the very best.

For some reason supermarkets seem to be a major battleground for public disruption. You can reduce this disruption by trying to prevent it in the first place.

- Have your children help you prepare by cutting coupons from the newspaper. Supervise the use of scissors.

- Have the children check the cupboards and refrigerator in helping you prepare your shopping list.
- Give your pocket calculator to the child who behaved best the last time you went out. He or she gets to add up the groceries as you call out the price.
- Have other children shop for the best price for the things on your shopping list.
- Have the children hunt for tough items to find. It's very handy to have such things as bay leaves, raisins, bouillon cubes or peppercorns on your shopping list.
- Give status and recognition to a child for pushing the cart through the aisles without clobbering somebody.

If you don't have the time, energy or patience to take these preventive steps, try these alternatives.

- Leave the kids with a baby-sitter or at grandma's house.
- Leave them with a friend and return the favor by doing her shopping for her. Then next week you can keep the kids and she can do your shopping.

If neither of these is possible and you have the kids with you and they make a fuss, here are some coping strategies.

- Leaving a child with no audience to witness a public tantrum is always your best first action.
- Another excellent suggestion is for parents with more than a little nerve. When your child first begins a tantrum, stand directly in front of him or her, look sternly into his or

her eyes and start whining just loud enough for the child to hear. Keep it up until the child quits fussing and starts looking at you, wondering what's wrong. Then firmly say, "Hush!"

- One mother told me of this coping mechanism. When her active 6-year-old just wouldn't stop running all around the store, she invented a loose-fitting strap attached to a rope. She took it out of the glove compartment just before entering the store and said, "If you don't settle down when I tell you to, I'll put this halter on you like you were a wild horse." The boy of course immediately tested her and, as she started to fit the halter on him, he said, "Don't, Mom. I'll be good." She never had to use it again.
- Remind the child that he or she will get a double penalty of standing in the corner when you get home if he or she doesn't hush up immediately.

Whatever strategy you employ to deal with the supermarket uproar, avoid these actions. They only make matters worse.

- Never slap the child across the face. I know some mothers who paddle the child's rear a couple of times. However, they only have to do it once. See the chapter on Spanking for more information.
- Never give in to children and buy a treat in order to make them be quiet. In giving a treat, timing is crucial. To make a treat an *incentive* rather than a *bribe*, give the child the treat *after* he or she has been quiet and cooperative for a few minutes. You want to reward responsibility, not disruption.

- If you bend over and lecture a screaming child about the virtues of compliance, you're wasting precious time and patience.

Restaurants are another place where children experiment with driving you crazy. To prevent disruption in a restaurant, make a little effort before the screaming starts.

- Keep a plastic catsup bottle, mustard container or salt shaker with colored beads in the car's glove compartment. Take one or more of these "playthings" into the restaurant to set on the table just as the child reaches to play with the real thing.
- Ask the waitress, host or hostess to bring you crayons and paper. Or, bring these items with you.
- You can avoid one headache by *not* dressing the children in their Sunday finest unless they have a proven record of good eating habits.
- I would love to see parents encourage certain types of restaurants to create a children's dining room so that everyone would have a more peaceful meal.

If your prevention efforts don't work and you're faced with screaming or fussing children in a restaurant, please don't let it continue.

- Abruptly leave the child at the table, walk halfway to the door and stop. Walk slowly back and say, "If you don't hush, we are leaving."
- After failing in this attempt, either send the child to the car if it's warm enough and he or

she is old enough, or simply leave the restaurant.
- You could also use the technique of doubling a punishment when you get home.
- Whatever you choose to do, *don't scream*, lecture or otherwise try to stop a public tantrum with a tantrum of your own.

If your child is disruptive when you are visiting friends or family, please don't be intimidated and let the child get away with it.

- Follow the same procedure you would use if you were at home. Standing the child in the corner or sitting him or her on a chair are preferred.
- For younger children or children who test you with public disruption for the first time, take them into another room and say, "If you continue your disruption, I will stand you in the corner just as if we were at home. So if you don't want that to happen, be quiet." Use the bathroom corner.

If your friends or family are critical of your actions, give them a lesson in responsible parenting.

- In front of everyone say, "Just because I come to your house (you come to my house) doesn't mean that I quit being a parent."
- If you face continued disapproval, maybe you should reevaluate your friendship or reduce the contact with those particular members of your family.

Runaway

When a child runs away from home, something is wrong. It might be that the child has been spoiled for many years and, when you finally decide to crack down, he or she views you as being overly punitive. The problem may lie in child abuse or in severe marital distress that has engulfed the child. Many children run away because they act on the impulses of anger, fear or revenge. Still other children leave home on the spur of the moment because they have falsely concluded that they are ready to meet the challenges of the grown-up world.

Whatever the cause, runaways must be found and the problem solved. The older the child, the more help you will probably need in achieving these goals. As you can tell from my PRESCRIPTIONS, I advise you to take action first and talk later.

First, control your emotions so that you can make the best decisions for your child.

- If you think you must, rant and rave for a few minutes to clear your emotions. Then set your feelings aside and solve the problem.
- Call somebody whom you trust not to gossip. This source of objective help might be a clergyman, a relative or a special friend. This confidant can help you with the other steps.

Second, locate your child and see him (her) to safety.

- If running away is the result of a small child's self-assertion, locating him (her) may simply call for you to keep an eye on the child as he or she walks down the street. If he (she) keeps going, follow, saying, "I just want to make sure you're all right. I'll leave you alone when you get settled." This technique permits you to supervise the child as it gives the child ample opportunity to change his (her) mind.
- Once you discover a runaway, call the child's best friend(s). Ask them politely but firmly to help you locate your child. It's best not to threaten them. They probably know all about the runaway, and explaining your serious parental concerns is the best way to elicit their cooperation.
- After receiving all possible information, call the police and give them a comprehensive report. Don't wait too long before taking this step. The sooner the police know everything that you know, the quicker they can respond to your need.
- Go hunting for the child yourself. You may not find him (her), but the activity will help you feel better. Ask the friend who is helping

you to stay by the phone, and you stay in touch with him (her).

- Give your child's friend(s) the National Runaway Hot Line phone number that applies in your area. To find this number, call 1-800-555-1212 and give the operator your area code. He or she will give you the hot line number for your area of the country. Tell the friend(s) to give the number to your child. You might say, "Kids on the run are in extreme danger. If you're my child's friend, at least have him (her) talk to someone at this number."

Third, upon locating the child, your first few words can be critical to future relations. After expressing your concern, try one of these:

- "I guess you're trying to tell me that something is wrong. I hear you loud and clear. How about giving me a chance to respond?"
- "I'll be willing to find out what I'm doing wrong in our family if you will do the same. Just because I'm your parent doesn't mean that I am always right."
- "Hey, we have problems to solve as a family and we can't do it if you're not here."

Finally, resolve to uncover what caused the child to run away and correct any problems.

- Let the child know from the beginning that the entire family will probably see a counselor. Just make sure you don't tell the child that all the problems are in his (her) head.

Sadness

Sadness can come and go in your child's life like the wind. It calls for you to remain steady, offering support and understanding. Most children have a marvelous ability to forget the hurt and get on with living. However, there are times when the sadness lingers, giving you the distinct impression that something is seriously wrong. This difficult time is complicated by the fact that if you give a sad child pity or special treats, he or she could get the notion that sadness can be used to manipulate people.

Dealing with a sad child is tricky. You want to give the child support without accidentally teaching him or her that sadness can be the beginning of a con job. My PRESCRIPTIONS will help you approach a child's sadness in such a way that you give the child support without getting trapped.

Before saying too much, you ought to take a look at the child's daily pattern of behavior. Here are some ques-

tions that will help you evaluate the severity of the sadness.

- Has the child stopped laughing and joking?
- Are there significant changes in the child's eating habits?
- Have there been dramatic changes in the child's personality?
- Does the child make remarks reflecting despair? For example, "Nothing is fun anymore," or "Life is just crummy."
- Is there indication of general jumpiness, restlessness or uncharacteristic outbursts or temper?
- Is the child withdrawing from activities, hobbies, etc., that you know the child really enjoys?
- Has the child stopped seeing old friends?
- Does the child ever start crying for no particular reason?
- Does the child complain of physical problems, but your doctor can't find anything wrong?
- If you answer yes to only one or two of these questions, chances are the sadness is minor and will pass. But if you're not confident of your evaluation, you probably should say something to the child.

If you decide to talk to your child about his or her sadness, don't be surprised if you don't get much information. Here are some words to use that might help open the door to a sharing of feelings.

- "I'm concerned about your sadness. You probably don't think that talking will solve anything but it's a marvelous place to start."

- "I've noticed some things that concern me [specify the behaviors you have observed *without* being critical]. If you want to talk about it, I'll help any way I can."
- "I see your bad feelings. If you want to share them, I'm here."
- If your child is acting as if his or her sadness excuses disruption, you might say, "I know you feel bad and you have a right to personal pain. But you also have the responsibility to control that pain so that it doesn't mess up the rest of your life."
- If your child is usually quite responsible and goes through a tough time, you might say, "I understand that these are tough days for you. I'll help you with your jobs for a couple of days."

Here are a few other things to keep in mind.

- Sadness becomes more complicated the older the child becomes. What might be minor at age 9 becomes more worrisome at age 17.
- Keep a special eye peeled for indication of drinking and/or drugs when teenagers are sad.
- Other possible signs of sadness can be biting fingernails, loss of concentration at school and various sleep disturbances.
- If the child won't talk, don't force it.
- If these hints don't help much, and you are still convinced something is wrong, you talk to someone to find out how you can help your child.
- Check out my PRESCRIPTIONS in the chapter on Seeking Professional Help.

School

Sending children to school is rough on parents. There are time-consuming schedules, never-ending chauffeuring and car pooling, and a constant need for supervision and involvement. Then there's the guilt you feel when you realize that sometimes you are glad that the kids are gone for six or seven hours; and, toward the end of summer, you can't wait for the school bells to chime once more.

Added to these pressures is the reality that your kids will probably have some problems adjusting to school. I think you should be somewhat pleased about this fact; there *is* a silver lining to the clouds that surround school problems. Your kids need to experience some problems outside the home. How else will they learn to handle the ups and downs that are a natural part of living? Most kids I know don't learn from their parents' mistakes. (Unfortunately). They're independent minded and usually must learn from their own hard knocks.

Once you respect your child's right to have problems,

you are better prepared to help him or her profit from difficult experiences. The only confusion with helping your children is that you never know for certain when your involvement and desire to help becomes interference. And, conversely, you must realize that giving children too much space to handle their own problems can become an excuse for indifference.

I believe there is a way to avoid the extremes of interference and indifference. The following PRESCRIPTIONS will help you find a rational balance between parental involvement and a child's right to independence as your kids are confronted with school problems.

I must suggest one hard-and-fast rule: *If at all possible, give your children a chance to solve their own problems before you step in.*

Communicating with school personnel, especially if your child has a problem, can be very touchy. Go slow and easy.

- Even if you want to talk with the coach or a special education teacher, give your child's main teacher the opportunity to know what's going on, just in case he (she) doesn't.
- It's good to keep in mind that, although professionally trained, educators are part of a bureaucratic system that often subjects professionals to unbelievable (and often unrealistic) pressures. So have some empathy.
- Call for an appointment. Such courtesy encourages mutual respect.
- Always let the principal know that you're at school. Check in at the school's office before seeing the teacher.
- Keep your comments concrete. Give and receive information that is specific. You will reach a workable solution quicker. Thus, if

the teacher says your child is "nervous and edgy," kindly ask him (her) to give you a recent example of what "nervous" means. If you find yourself saying, "My child is very sensitive," rephrase your statement, giving the teacher a concrete example of what you mean by "sensitive."

- If you make any suggestions, don't sound cocky or aloof; it'll backfire on you and your child. If you want to give the teacher a suggestion that he or she might use to help your child, try these words of introduction: "I read somewhere that a teacher tried . . ."
- Write down any resolution or results that require you, the teacher, or another person to take some remedial action.
- Keep the child in the middle of your discussion. In some cases, you may invite the child to join you *after* the discussion passes over any difficulties. This shows respect for the child and saves you the time and energy of interpreting what was said to the child. For example, if you and the teacher decide that the child must do at least an hour of homework each school night, bring the child into the room and *both* of you explain the whys and wherefores of this recommendation.
- If there are any changes to be made, agree to a time during which you will review the child's progress and evaulate the impact of any changes.
- Through the process, don't get threatened. You don't cause the child's school problems; he or she does. If you keep a level head you can best figure out how to help the child. Anyway, your children may have trouble at school and not at home.

If your child is having trouble with a teacher ("Mrs. Miller always picks on me," or, the teacher is constantly writing bad reports despite the conferences you've had), and you believe the child has tried his or her best to stay out of the doghouse, you may have to intervene.

- Confront the teacher first before going to the administration.
- Call for an appointment, inform the principal of a possible problem, and do your best to convey continued respect to the teacher.
- Begin the confrontation by reviewing your notes of the past conferences (see hint above). You might say, "I have a problem. I think my child has tried to correct [the problem discussed previously] but things are still troublesome. Do you think we have a problem?"
- If the teacher remains rational, continue by specifying your view. Don't call him or her names or take cheap shots ("A good teacher would know how to resolve this problem").
- If there is no resolution of the problem, tell the teacher that you will be requesting a meeting with the principal and you invite him or her to join you.
- Follow through immediately, but don't invite the teacher again; let the principal exercise some options in this regard.
- When talking with the principal, follow the same hints of courtesy suggested above.
- Do your best to work things out with the principal. But don't be afraid to ask the principal for a meeting with the appropriate administrator in the school district's central office. If you stay rational, the principal should do his or her best to resolve any problems at the local level.

To give you a comprehensive list of helpful hints dealing with underachievement would take a special book. Even then, you might not have the final answer. When faced with failure, all you can do is give it your best shot. That's what I'm going to do with my hints.

- Pay close attention to younger children's learning habits. If they get a bad grade, help them concentrate on *how* to solve the problem, not on getting the right answer.
- Grades are important but don't overdo their importance. Praise improvement more than A's and B's.
- If you decide to pay for certain grades or a percentage improvement, make the payment a part of a comprehensive program. Check pages 110 through 117 of my book, *Keeping Parents Out of Trouble*.
- Rely on the teachers and school psychologists to alert you to any substantial problem. Don't be afraid to ask for a conference on this issue if you're not sure.
- If you want to start a program of improvement, make it *gradual*. Review papers daily or at least weekly to decide whether or not improvement is occurring.
- If you punish the child for poor grades, keep the punishment short and get it over with. For example, ground the child for the weekend with no phone or friends rather than grounding him or her until the end of the grading period, which may be several weeks away.
- To guard against cheating, complete a random check of the papers your child is bringing home. Call the teacher and find out if the paper your child brought home is the same one that the teacher sent.

- Parental need for achievement or frustration over the perceived lack of same can cause excessive pressure on kids to perform. Ask yourself whether or not you are trying to relive your life through your children.

A child can disrupt a class in a hundred different ways. Talking out of turn, pestering a classmate, passing notes or just plain doing nothing are frequent complaints of teachers. Your role is to help the teacher help your child.

- *First offense.* Let the school take care of the penalty. Remind the child that if it happens again, he or she will receive a double penalty, one from the school and one from you. Don't specify what you might do.
- *Second offense.* In addition to the school's penalty, implement a strong grounding (two nights at home with no TV, radio and phone).
- *Third offense.* Repeat as in second offense, only make the grounding for a weekend. In addition, do what one mother found very helpful; after clearing it with the principal and teacher, walk unannounced into your child's classroom and sit in the back of the room for about five minutes, then leave. When your child asks you about it, simply reply, "You've been acting up in class. I tried punishing you but it didn't work. The only thing left for me to do is to help the teacher make you mind."
- *Repeated disruption.* Request a referral to the school psychologist.
- If the problem is good old-fashioned laziness, ask the teacher to send incomplete

work home and you make the child finish the work before playing.

- If you decide to try a reinforcement program in which you pay for improved conduct, you'll need the teacher(s) to give you daily feedback on the specific behavior to be improved. Research suggests that the best way to achieve overall improvement is for the reward to be given at the end of the day rather than after each class. For older children (junior high), the reward should be given at the end of the week.

Just about every kid will skip school or a class sometime. You need not hit the ceiling, but see that something is done about it.

- No matter what the circumstances, make it clear to the school officials that you want to be notified in case of truancy. Tell the proper authority that you prefer a phone call rather than a letter.
- If it's a minor offense, like a first-time class tardy slip, you need not take punitive action. However, you should make certain that the school enforces its policy on tardiness. Also let the child know that you know what happened. You might say, "I know you were late to class. Let me know if I can be of help."
- If you learn of a minor offense long after the fact, don't get upset. If your child seriously abuses school regulations and educators know that you want to know, believe me—they'll tell you.
- If your child skips a class or school for the first time, your action at home should depend upon the child's overall level of

responsibility. Using the scale in the chapter on Responsibility, determine the child's responsibility in the last month. If it's in the upper levels, you may decide to let the child off with this warning, "You've been very responsible lately so I'll give you a break. Just don't try it again."

If the child's responsibility has been only fair, you should impose at least some degree of grounding.

- If your child is regularly truant and you've tried various types of grounding with no success, you probably have a situation on your hands that calls for professional consultation.

I can't possibly cover all the school situations that might require your involvement. But here are a few of the ones I've encountered most often.

Bully.

- Being nonviolent, I hate to say this, but there could come a time when your child would have to defend himself or herself from a bully by using physical force. This is a scary thing for a child, so control your empathic anger until he or she has cleared this hurdle. Of course, remind the child to try talking and walking before hitting.
- If you ever supervise a bully, research suggests that making him or her play alone and physically apart from the group for ten to fifteen minutes before returning to the group is effective.
- Bully-type behaviors tend to go down when children engage in positive sharing experi-

ences (show and tell, cooperative games, helping-each-other projects).

- My experience indicates that it's best to avoid hard-line competitive games when there are bullies involved. So you may want to temporarily pull your child out of the baseball, football or soccer game if the coach can't or won't control a bully.
- To parents of a bully: bullying is an indication of deeper problems. Take an honest look at the environment in your home; recheck the chapter on Positive Family Activity (P.F.A.). Reevaluate your manners as well as the child's. Also look to the less frequent causes. I've seen cases when a "bully" actually had juvenile diabetes, a learning disability or was being abused in some way. Find out what's going on behind the scenes.

School Bus.

- Bus drivers should be seen as legitimate authority figures and children should be expected to conform to rules and regulations while riding the bus.
- Support any program that seeks to train bus drivers in proper disciplinary procedures.

Boarding School.

- I personally don't approve of children going to elementary boarding schools. At these early ages, they need daily exposure to a primary family unit.
- There are special circumstances that might suggest children be placed in a secondary boarding school environment. This should

be done because it is the best thing for the child, not for parental convenience.
- I personally don't like to see a child attend all four years of a secondary boarding school, unless he or she absolutely wants to and/or there are ample opportunities for the child to mix with the opposite sex.
- I believe that a child should have a complete work-up done, including vocational counseling, before being enrolled in a boarding school.

Special Education.

- If your child has a learning disability or other condition that makes his or her education "special," give all the help you possibly can, but do not feel sorry for the child. Children with special education problems already have an uphill battle; they don't need the extra burden of overcoming pity.
- See that the child's special needs are being met by a teacher(s) who has good qualifications and is completely informed as to the child's deficiency. Ask for a staff conference whenever there is significant change in the child's status.

Medical Screening.

- Allergies, refined-sugar overdose or other physiological problems often underlie behavior problems. Before seeking psycho-educational consultation, eliminate the possibility of physiological problems by seeing that the child has a thorough medical screening.

Seeking Professional Help

Most people find it very distressing to admit that they can't handle their personal affairs. Seeking help with personal problems seems to be tantamount to admitting that you have a few screws loose and aren't fit for the human race. Yet, if we take a long, hard look in the mirror, we have to see that we are *all* a little goofy, if for no other reason than trying to live in today's crazy world would drive anybody nuts.

Another cause of people's reluctance to seek help is the guarded professionalism of some therapists. While it is true that counselors need to maintain an emotional distance from their clients or patients, many professionals use this guideline as an invitation to look down their noses at people in pain. In so doing, these therapists pretend that they are the only truly sane persons. And that *is* screwy.

There's no reason that therapists can't be warm, kind and even humble in working with people who need help. Just because therapists are knowledgeable about how people function doesn't necessarily mean that they aren't a little nutty like the rest of us.

If you have the need for help, don't be a passive victim to the insensitivities or bland generalities of any professional helper. In fact, if you just sit there and do nothing when you encounter a therapist who makes no sense at all, then I suggest that your first problem to solve is your lack of self-assertion. Use these PRESCRIPTIONS when seeking professional help.

Knowing when to seek help can be as confusing as finding the right helper.

You ought to seek help when:

- A confidant tells you that you need more help than the friendly advice he or she can give.
- You've tried all sorts of rewards and punishments with your children but nothing seems to work.
- You experience a trauma (runaway, divorce, child is pregnant or jailed) and don't know which way to turn.
- A big problem repeats itself. Your child constantly abuses alcohol or other drugs, hits you, stays out all night or absolutely refuses to stay grounded when so instructed.
- You reach a frustration level at which you have little or no mental energy or patience left. You have that end-of-the-rope feeling.
- You don't have a big problem, but you are bothered by lack of confidence and/or skills in parenting. One or two prevention sessions can be well worth the time and expense.

Getting the name of a reputable counselor/therapist

who most likely will help you with your problem is difficult. Try one or more of the following.

- Talk to trusted friends and see whom they might recommend.
- Ask the school counselor, dean of students or local probation officer about counselors who are known to work well with children and families.
- Call your local youth agency and ask for a referral.
- Talk to your clergyman or pediatrician about a referral.
- If none of these work, check your Yellow Pages for ethical advertising or a referral-service phone number.

Knowing how to evaulate a potential counselor/therapist is also tough. Here are a few hints of what to look for.

- A reputable counselor/therapist will be a professionally trained and duly licensed psychologist, psychiatrist, social worker, marriage counselor, clergyman or other social scientist working for a reputable agency. You don't necessarily have to seek out a particular type of counselor/therapist as long as you follow the suggestions I've already given you.
- A qualified helper should be able to outline his or her approach to counseling. Ask for a brief description of the helper's theoretical viewpoint and be satisfied that you agree with the helper's philosophy.
- Don't expect to get much information over the phone prior to the first appointment. Any

reputable counselor/therapist will want to talk with you in person before outlining his or her approach.

- Within two or three days after the first appointment, some of the things the counselor/therapist said should make sense to you. If nothing makes sense, you ought to reevaluate your choice of counselors/therapists.
- As for the counseling/therapy dichotomy, some helpers suggest that therapy is more intensive than counseling. When seeking professional help, I don't think the dichotomy makes any difference.

Beware of certain realities that can be harsh when they are not clarified.

- Make it clear that you're not relinquishing control over your family just because you're having problems. Some counselors or agencies tend to fall into the trap of overextending their authority. Remember, helpers are consultants to your life, not masters over it.
- Ask about confidentiality, especially if any report of services is to be forwarded to another person or agency.
- Be ready to invest energy, time and money in counseling/therapy. Most counselors/therapists seek more than money from their profession, but, if they're good, they should be paid well for what they do.
- Have a clear understanding of fees, payment schedules and the applicability of your insurance before the first appointment. Counseling/therapy is expensive (even if you pay on a sliding scale), and you don't want money standing between you and the help you need.

There are other things you can do to find someone to talk to. Try one or more of the following. But keep in mind that, if you have a very difficult problem, you still may need to talk to a professional.

- Join a self-help group. Many cities have tens or even hundreds of such groups that can prove very helpful.
- Call local hot lines that specialize in talking to people in distress.
- Or call a national hot line by dialing 1-800-555-1212 and asking the operator if he or she has the number of a service that will help you with your problem (describe it briefly to the operator).
- Seek out various support groups within your church or temple.
- In certain areas of the country, local radio talk shows feature a psychologist who will try to help you find a direction with your problem. A few of these areas are: Los Angeles, Detroit, Washington, D.C., Boston, Atlanta and Seattle.
- Advise your child to join a teen group at church, the YM or YWCA or a self-help group for young people.

Sex

Parents usually get nervous about sexual issues. I don't pretend that my recommendations will alleviate your nervousness or solve the potential problems. Sex is such a private affair that I don't think any parent can "solve" a child's sexual concerns. You can, however, follow some rational guidelines in passing along reasonable moral standards while you protect your children from any sexual hang-ups you may still experience.

Many kids as well as grown-ups falsely believe that sexuality begins when you touch another person. Not so.

- Sexuality begins when people talk to, not touch, one another. It is critically important that kids learn how to feel relaxed in talking with boys (girls).
- Encourage preteens to play cooperative games and engage in light-hearted discussions.

- Actively discourage any sexual stereotyping in either sex. For example, consider these falsehoods: Boys don't cry; girls shouldn't be sports minded; boys have to be mean; girls don't assert themselves.

Don't let children overplay their sex role. They may think they are cute, but they can get in over their heads.

- Limit makeup, provocative clothing and other sexual cues that often convey more than the child is ready to handle.
- If your physically mature daughter is giving a "come-on" to strange boys, don't overreact. Explain to her that she may be giving the boys a message that she's not aware of.

Sex education programs aren't always as reliable as they should be. Solid information is essential to satisfactory sexual adjustment.

- Don't be fooled by a child's all-knowing attitude. Even though you may have a sophisticated teenager, he or she could have many misconceptions about sex.
- One mother told me that she is able to talk candidly about sexual issues with her daughter while she (Mom) is driving the car. With her eye on the road, the mother talks to her daughter without subjecting the kid to the potential embarrassment of direct eye contact.
- Many kids don't profit from sex education classes because they don't want to appear stupid by asking questions or acting interested. By pretending to be informed, they often miss information.

- Here are three excellent books that will greatly help you in your sex ed efforts.

  For the young child, *Where Did I Come From*, by Peter Mayle, Lyle Stuart Publishers, 1973. A Light-hearted look, complete with excellent illustrations, at the fundamental answer to the question posed by the title.

  For the preteen/teenager, *What's Happening to Me?*, by Peter Mayle, Lyle Stuart Publishers, 1975. A light-hearted look at the central issues of puberty.

  For kids ages 10–11 and beyond, *Changing Bodies, Changing Lives*, by Ruth Bell, et al., Random House, 1980. An in-depth look at every conceivable issue relating to the second decade of life. If you buy only one book, make it this one.

You must assume the role of censor regarding sex in the movies and on television.

- If there is a question about a show involving sexuality and you don't know what is presented, you should disapprove of the child watching it *unless* he or she is willing to tell you what was seen and what he or she thinks about it.
- Sexuality in movies and on television can afford you an excellent opportunity to discuss the issues with your children. By commenting upon unrealistic aspects, you have a chance to give your kids your views. Keep your eyes peeled for such misleading ideas as: Women are sexy only if they play dumb roles; big breasts automatically mean sexual fulfillment; men must be tough and macho

in order to be sexy; if men don't conquer women, then there's something wrong.

Although much has been written about the acceptability of masturbation, many parents still get nervous about this subject.

- Masturbation is quite natural. This tongue-in-cheek statistic says it well: 98 percent of boys admit they masturbate; the other 2 percent lie about it. In addition, masturbation by girls is perfectly acceptable.
- Masturbation is a perfect way for people to explore their sexual fantasies and coping strategies. Kids are always sexy and competent in their masturbatory fantasies.
- Nocturnal emissions or "wet dreams" are also quite normal. Kids who wake up with semen on the sheets or a wet vagina should know that wet dreams are a natural occurrence.
- Pornography will probably be part of a kid's masturbation. Don't get upset if your kid has material that shows provocative nudity or heterosexual activity. Just remind him or her to keep it in a private place. You're better off not making a big deal out of a copy of *Playboy*, *Playgirl* or *Penthouse*.
- If you should accidentally walk in on your child's masturbation, apologize and leave. Later, make a simple, unemotional statement to the effect that the kid should protect his or her privacy better by locking doors, etc.

Dating is very important. Consider these helpful hints when this critical time comes along.

- You might permit chaperoned dating at 14 or

15. Unchaperoned dating probably shouldn't begin until 16. Exceptions might be made in the case of a responsible kid and a big event like the homecoming dance.

- Once your kids reach 11 or 12, you might approve "boyfriends/girlfriends" visiting your house. Remind the child that this is a "friend" and not a date.

Trusting your children in sexual matters is very difficult. Here are a few guidelines that should make things easier for all.

- Be honest about your lack of trust. It could help stimulate a profitable discussion during which you can learn how mature your kid is and he or she can learn what you're worried about.
- When kids display responsibility in key areas—chores, school, temper control, manners, curfew, financial control—you can be more confident that they will exercise responsibility in sexual matters. As I often tell parents, *responsibility is contagious, so is sloppiness.*
- Probably the most important issue in trusting your children in matters of sexuality is *how much they trust you.* Are you the kind of responsible authority figure to whom they can turn when they are confused about life? Have you proven that you mean what you say? Have you shown that the values you espouse are solid enough that you follow them? If you can answer Yes to these questions, then your children will most likely turn to you if and when they need help.

When parents don't trust their kids in sexual matters,

certain problems surface that sound legitimate, but are actually mistrust in disguise. If any of these sound familiar, use my hint to speak your mind.

- Do you really have to wear that? It just doesn't look right." Try this question instead. "Do you realize that you look very sexy? I'm not certain that you are ready to handle the reactions of other kids."
- "You've been out too late recently. I want you home at 9 P.M." What you really might need to say is, "I'm really worried about you going out with a boy I haven't met. Please have him come in for a moment."
- "Why can't you go out with 'the boys' ('the girls') sometimes?" Is this on your mind? "I'm scared that you're getting too close to your boyfriend (girlfriend) and you won't control your sexual impulses. Could you possibly ease my mind a little?"
- "I don't like you dating that older boy (girl), it doesn't look right." A more honest reaction might be, "I'm worried that your older date might use you in a bad way without caring for you. I would hurt badly for you if that happened."

Many parents sooner or later encounter the awkward moment of catching a son or daughter in the heat of passion. Now what?

- Control your emotions so that you don't blurt something out that you'll regret later.
- Ask the child to restore his or her composure and leave the area.
- Before too much time goes by (the next day), talk to your kid in private about his or her control of passion. Be glad the kid felt com-

fortable to let his or her hair down at home (if that's where it was).
- Don't tell your friends or the other kids about the incident; it's nobody's business.

If you find out that your child is sexually active, go slow.

- It will do you no good to attack the kid. The key strategy at this point is to assure yourself that the kid recognizes the seriousness of his or her decision.
- Make certain that the kid knows that trust, sharing, good communication, ease of self-expression, mutual kindness and honesty are more important to sexuality than who touches whom, where and how.
- Be assured that your kid and his or her friend are fully briefed on contraceptive practices. Suggest that *both* of them visit a family planning center.
- Let your kid know that while you don't expect to interfere in his or her sexual practices, you *do* expect him or her to exercise more maturity and responsibility in daily matters. Hence, in order for the kid to date regularly, he or she must continue getting good grades, helping around the house and doing other things that reflect mature self-control.
- I've talked with many parents who, after they've gotten over the shock, have invited their child and his or her friend to a rather serious and highly private discussion. *Without sarcasm*, these parents have expressed their honest feelings including that they disapprove but will not attempt to stop the kids from seeing each other.

I have agreed with this procedure since the seriousness of the discussion and the parental honesty do more to warn the kids of the dangers than all the lectures in the world.

Kids who are dating need to know about sexually transmitted diseases. STDs is the catchall category used instead of venereal disease.

- STDs are rapidly increasing due to many things. Among the factors contributing to their spread are kids not communicating with each other about their sexual experiences, the idea that these diseases somehow make a kid bad, reluctance of sexually active kids to seek medical examinations and increased use of the pill with less utilization of condoms and foams.
- Kids should know that STDs can be spread from one person to another through kissing, heavy petting and oral sex as well as through intercourse.
- If the kids are concerned about the possibility of contracting an STD, they should take their sex partner and go *together* to a VD clinic. Going together gives them support and reduces the embarrassment.
- If both kids have sex *only* with each other, they can worry less about STDs.
- Vaginal foams and condoms aid in avoiding STDs.
- The warning signs are clearly outlined and discussed in the book, *Changing Bodies, Changing Lives*, referred to earlier.
- If your child should happen to contract an STD, forget the preaching; just make certain

he or she is immediately seen by a doctor or treated at a reputable medical facility.

- Your child should know *ahead of time* that if he or she contracts an STD, he or she must press the sex partner to go to a clinic or private doctor.
- If your child doesn't have the nerve to talk about it or is afraid of people finding out, he or she can call the National VD Hot Line. The best way to get the most useful phone number is to call the toll-free information operator, 1-800-555-1212, and ask for the VD Hot Line in your area of the country.
- If you have a discussion with your child and his or her sex partner, the helpful hints contained in this section represent the kind of information you can talk about.

Sibling Rivalry

When children fight with each other over toys, bathroom privileges, and who-said-what-to-whom, parents often wish that one of the kids was an only child. The noise and fighting so often a part of sibling rivalry force parents to take some type of action.

The temptation to get in the middle and "take charge" of the situation is overwhelming. Many parents get absorbed in the "amateur shrink" routine, attempting to analyze why the sibling rivalry occurs in the first place. Taking charge is fine, provided the kids learn a lesson from the altercation. While playing the shrink role might help you work toward long-term change, it does little to stop the disruption *now*.

From my view, it's not the parents' responsibility to prevent sibling rivalry; that's the kids' job. However, parents must give their children the tools and motivation that will allow them to solve their problems and learn to live with one another.

When you intervene in a sibling fight, make it short and don't play detective. Start out slow and take as strong an action as needed.

- With minor altercations or "normal" rivalry, simply say, "Stop it!"
- Resist all temptations to step into the middle and figure out who started it and who should shoulder the blame. It won't work.
- When the children are under 10 years of age and Stop it! doesn't work, stand both of them in the corner for ten minutes. See the chapter on The Reward of Punishment for more details.
- Research suggests that an excellent way of handling two kids who fight with each other is to sit both of them on opposite sides of *the same room* and make each of them play with a game or toy without interacting with each other. You should supervise this solitary play for 10 or 15 minutes two or three times a day. Teenagers who fight should be made to play a friendly game at the kitchen table for 30 minutes.
- If kids are arguing over a possession, take it away from both of them and say, "You can have it back when you learn to play together."
- Be willing to sit with two *rational* children and mediate a dispute. Point out how each might compromise with the other in order to get along better.
- REMEMBER: the thing that often keeps sibling rivalry going is your taking sides, paying attention to a particular child. Thus, the child who "lost" your support will likely institute another argument in hopes of "winning" you back to his or her side.

Kids often choose a lousy time to fight. One of the worst times for sibling fights to crop up is when you're in the car.

- Give the kids a lesson in the importance of brothers and sisters being friends by saying, "If you guys don't start being friendly, you won't see your other friends for two days."
- If you don't like this action or it doesn't work, pull over to the side of the road and say, "Either the fighting leaves the car or both of you will."
- If they test you on this warning and you're not on a superhighway, pull over to the side of the road, ask them to get out, slam the door and sit there for ten seconds. Then, open the door and say, "Get in and be quiet."
- If this doesn't work, you probably have problems that go deeper than simple sibling rivalry. You'll need help sorting them out.

Fights involving one child having an unfair advantage over the other calls for careful intervention.

- Adopt the role of referee, saying to the child with the advantage, "You have an unfair advantage. If you continue your attack, I'll be forced to make things more even."
- A few examples of making things even would be:
    1. Tying one arm of a bigger child behind the back prior to letting the kids wrestle.
    2. If both children can swim, making the two kids finish their argument in a swimming pool; water is a great equalizer.

3. Giving a weaker child a headstart in a competitive event.

Role reversal is a time-consuming, but often effective, technique for teaching siblings to get along with each other.

- Separate feuding kids and coax them to "play a game" with you. Tell them you want them to practice being movie stars.
- Tell each child that you want him or her to play the part of his or her brother/sister.
- Have them physically switch places before you start the game.
- Start the action with one child verbally attacking the other. Once they know what their first lines are (have them rehearse), call out, "Action!"
- The kids will slip back into their own roles very quickly. You must stop the action, reorient them to their new roles and repeat, "Action."
- It won't take more than one or two interchanges for the lesson to take effect. Then you can point out to them how it feels to be in the other guy's shoes. This empathic experience can nip sibling rivalry in the bud.

Positive prevention strategies can be used to stop sibling rivalry before it gets a solid foothold in your family.

- Make each child responsible for suggesting (or even organizing) a Positive Family Activity (see earlier chapter). The child should receive a special status within the family for contributing to the welfare of all.
- Inducing younger siblings to play cooperatively with the same game or toy can reduce the inclination to fight.

Single Parenting

The toughest part of single parenting is that you have to raise your children without moral support. Common uncertainties suddenly take on a more awesome quality. "Am I doing what's best for my children? Will they be okay? Will not having a mother (father) cause permanent damage?"

Left unanswered, these questions can quickly erode the confidence of a single parent. But take heart. As a single parent, you may not have the best of all possible worlds, but it's certainly better than being trapped in a bad marriage.

Single parents need support. Here are a few Prescriptions *for developing a support system.*

- Give yourself at least thirty minutes a day to take time out from "the rat race." When you *first* get home from work, ask the children to give you a few minutes to calm down. Take a shower, go jogging, soak in the tub or do whatever else helps you relax. When you do pay attention to the children, you'll be in better shape if you take care of yourself first.

- Develop a reliable system of baby-sitters. For more information, see the chapter entitled "Baby-sitters and Day Care."
- Consider joining a local support group. Families Anonymous, Parents without Partners, or groups associated with your local church or college might prove helpful.
- Talk regularly with a friend about your child-rearing efforts.
- Read at least two books a year on child rearing.

The following guidelines apply to all families, but especially those involving single parents.

- Write your rules down and post them.
- Use Stop it! as a tool to interrupt disruption. It doesn't necessarily prevent future disruption, but it can give you time to think about what to do next.
- Give the kids more opportunity to develop independence. Self-care in such areas as getting to bed and getting up, chores and preparing their own snacks can help you as well as the kids.
- Make a special effort not to nag, lecture or preach. See Appendix.
- Keep a diary of your children's positive and negative behaviors so that you have a somewhat objective source of referral in case you become concerned about your children's welfare. Then you can look back and see if a pattern has developed.
- Don't be afraid to seek professional consultation sooner than you might if you were married.

Dating is a complicated business for the single parent. Keep these hints in mind and then enjoy yourself.

- Let the kids know that you need special friends just as they do.
- Introduce your special friend to your children *after* he or she has taken on some degree of "specialness" to you.
- Once your children have greeted your friend, expect them to disappear.
- Keep sexual activity away from the eyes and ears of your kids.
- If your friend sleeps with you, expect him or her to leave before the children wake up.
- Once you believe that you have a relationship that will last for the foreseeable future, you may wish to permit your friend to be part of more family activities. Eventually, this might include breakfast.

Don't be surprised if your children use your single status to try to manipulate you. Here are some possible complaints and my suggestion for a good response.

"I wouldn't get into trouble if I had a father (mother)."
- "You do have a father (mother). And, as for trouble, you cause the trouble and you can stop it."

"You wouldn't get mad at me if you had a husband (wife)."
- "I get myself mad because I get angry at things *not* because I don't have a husband (wife)."

"If Dad (Mom) was here, I could have the things I want."
- "You might get more attention, but you wouldn't get any more things."

Spanking

Discipline is often equated with spanking. Yet spanking is just one of many disciplinary techniques. And it isn't the cure-all that many parents think it is. It may have been appropriate one hundred years ago when most of life's daily activities were grounded in physical survival. Given the "mental" nature of modern civilization, it seems sensible to work directly with the child's mind rather than relying upon physical aggression as a surefire attention-getting strategy.

I basically don't like spanking. Modern research on rewards and punishments has given us more sophisticated methods of giving children mental lessons without getting so physical. Hitting a child seems barbaric. Except for very specific situations, I would like to see spanking become an old-fashioned technique that is out of date.

Spanking can be the lesser of two evils. Keep these hints in mind when spanking children.

209

- Spanking is the best discipline when a child is about to endanger himself or herself. Running into the street, playing with a mean dog, or being about to fall out of a tree onto the concrete call for two or three swift pops on the rear.
- Spanking should be executed immediately. If you find yourself telling the child that he or she will be spanked later, I suggest that you use denial of privileges or restriction of freedom instead.
- If you spank too often, the child will become numb to the punishment and it will lose its effectiveness. If this happens, spanking won't work when you really want it to.
- No matter why you spank, gently pat the child two or three times after he or she has resumed appropriate activity. This compensates for being hit.
- One light pop on the rear can be used more as a startle technique than punishment. Getting a child's attention in this way can serve to make warnings more effective.
- By the time children reach their fifth birthday, try to find other disciplinary methods. Standing the child in the corner is good. See the chapter, The Reward of Punishment.
- In explaining spanking to young children, consider this idea: "I spanked you because I want your brain to remember that running into the street (touching the stove, playing with an electrical outlet) is dangerous."

Stealing

There's a giant soft spot in my heart that cringes when I write about children "stealing." I want to believe that only "criminals" steal. I'd like to say that children engage in "youthful pranks," or "harmless antics," not stealing. Yet when a 6-year-old swipes a piece of bubble gum from the store or a preteen takes a dollar from your wallet, what else do you call it? The child took something that wasn't his (hers). The verdict? The child is guilty of stealing.

We'd all like to call youthful stealing something that makes it sound better. But taking something that doesn't belong to you is stealing, pure and simple. Calling it something else doesn't help children learn an important lesson.

Stealing doesn't make children "bad." It simply means that for a moment they strayed from the path of morality and did a bad thing. They need help, not condemnation.

My PRESCRIPTIONS for stealing are similar to those for

lying and cheating. Keep in mind that the younger the child, the milder you can be in your discipline.

When you suspect stealing, here are the seven steps you should follow:

- Gather reliable evidence that you believe.
- Confront the child with the evidence.
- Permit the air to clear through catharsis.
- Help the child face the victim.
- Implement a punishment to fit the crime.
- Institute some type of restitution.
- Give the child a chance to re-earn his or her reputation.

Each step calls for some action. These hints can make the program just "prosecution," rather than unjust "persecution."

Gathering evidence.

- If you punish without adequate evidence, you run the risk of needless rebellion.
- One very reliable witness will give you confidence to proceed.
- I prefer that parents have a confession from the child before proceeding. Sometimes a direct confrontation with the witness or the threat of same will stimulate a full disclosure.
- Even if you lack adequate evidence, you can still proceed to step two.

Confronting the child.

- Sit privately with the child and present your evidence.
- Permit a rational response, but interrupt

lame excuses. You want the child's version of the story, not aimless accusations.

- At this stage, concentrate your efforts on whether or not the act was committed, not on the circumstances surrounding the act.
- Do *not* browbeat or shame the child.
- Steps two and three have some overlap, so you may end up bouncing back and forth between the two steps.

Permitting catharsis.

- Whether the evidence is reliable or not, the child will have an emotional reaction to the confrontation. While accusations and excuses lead nowhere, it is important to permit the child to have an emotional reaction. This may be fear, anger, resentment or a combination of these and other feelings.
- Accept a moderate degree of disgust and/or disappointment, whether experienced by you or your child.
- If emotions begin to dominate rationality, take time out from the procedure until tempers cool.
- The next three steps are time consuming and should only be taken if you are reasonably certain of the evidence.
- If you are *not* sure of the child's culpability, remind him or her that stealing will result in a punishment if ever you find strong evidence that he or she has committed such an act.

Facing the victim.

- The child must, if at all possible, face the victim and offer a formal apology.

- You should accompany the child so that you ensure that the child is appropriately admonished without being badgered by the victim. For the younger child (a 5-year-old who swipes a piece of candy), facing the store manager is probably punishment enough. After taking the child to the manager, forget the incident.

Implementing a punishment.

- Children should receive some penalty (at least in their minds).
- When handing out the punishment, consider the circumstances surrounding the crime; that is, the child's age, general level of responsibility, history of stealing, lying or cheating, and whether or not he or she gave you a confession.
- I recommend some type of restriction of freedom (grounding) and/or denial of privileges. This should last a few days for a 10-year-old to a week for a teenager.

Instituting restitution.

- Some act of restitution should be included in the disciplinary procedures for older kids (10 and above). This restitution is *in addition to* the penalty.
- Explanation of restitution should include the concept of paying the victim back for the insult of being ripped off.
- Examples of restitution are: working for the victim, paying the victim money that the child earned, and working for a charitable organization within the community.

Re-earning reputation.

- It wouldn't be a bad idea for *all* kids of any age to realize that your trust of them has slipped a little since their theft. You can do this by prohibiting normal freedoms for a day or two.

Stepparenting

Entering into a parenting role with someone else's children is kind of like tasting a new food. There's no way to know if you'll like it or not until you try it. Even though you spend a lot of time getting to know the child/children, the stepparent role doesn't really begin until you live with the child/children day in and day out.

"Stepping" is an adjustment for all concerned. If you are stepping or are considering it, make certain your new marriage is strong, your dedication lasting and your communication with your new spouse crisp and clear.

Here are a few guidelines that will get a new stepparent off on the right foot.

- Don't try to replace the natural parent. Be yourself and give the kids time to get to know the real you. Trying to be someone you're not will give the children reason to reject you.

- Don't try to win your stepchildren's love by spoiling them.
- Allow your spouse and his or her children to have some time alone, especially at the beginning of a relationship. This way, you don't force yourself on the kids and you give them time to learn to love you.
- Caution your new spouse (the kids' parent) *not* to ask for the children's approval of your relationship.
- Don't run down the child's natural parent, at least not in front of the child. This causes the child to defend his or her parent and forces him or her to choose between two people he or she loves.
- If you have children of your own, don't expect to love your stepchildren the same way you love your own. Chances are it won't happen.

As a stepparent, you will probably be compared with the child's natural parent in one way or another. Here are a few hints that will help you tolerate and understand those comparisons.

- Comparison is a difficult challenge to your self-confidence. When you face it, smile and realize that you will probably come out on the short end of a comparison without doing a thing wrong.
- Children who compare you to a natural parent may actually be *drawn to you.* They might feel uncomfortable in loving you because they think they can't love you as well as their natural parent. They reaffirm their natural parent's superiority and eliminate their own guilt by reminding themselves that

their parent does something better than you do.

- Comparisons can be tough on a new marriage. In a step situation, kids have a way of spotlighting negative traits in their natural parent (your spouse). For example, you can overlook your husband's sloppiness but when his kids spend a weekend following the example of their father, you may find yourself wondering, How come I haven't seen that trait in my husband? What else don't I know about this man?
SOLUTION: Say something to your spouse as soon as possible. Ask him to compensate for the trait at least while the kids are around.
- Your best response to being compared to a natural parent is: "I want you to love your Dad (Mom). But save some space to love me, too. There's plenty of room you know."

If you overcome the potential threat of comparisons, your objectivity can be an advantage in rearing stepchildren. You tend not to have the blind spots that so often afflict a natural parent.

- You can identify problem behaviors very quickly. Early intervention can prevent frustration from building and making the problems worse.
- Your disciplinary action is usually more efficient in that you take the needed action without argument. The sooner it's over with, the better.
- Your actions probably are less threatening to the child's self-esteem. The child is better able to see that you're simply dealing with a problem. Likewise, the child might feel freer

in sharing complicated or confusing information with you.

Here a few responses that will help you handle the trying times of being a stepparent.

- "I admit that I'm not your father (mother). But right now, I'm your parent and you must do as I say."
- "You can call me Dad (Mom) or Bill (Debbie), it's up to you."
- "I really don't want to hassle you, but if you don't obey our rules, I must do something to get your attention."
- "Your father (mother) and I need time alone. I want you to respect that."

Telephone

Rather than become frustrated at your child's tendency to talk on the phone instead of sleeping or eating, take heart. You have at your disposal a great tool with which to teach responsibility. However, you must stay tough in setting and enforcing rules concerning telephone use. Keep the responsibility on your children. At the same time, maintain flexibility concerning phone use. It's a fantastic instrument, but make it work for, not against, you.

Rules concerning phone use should be adapted to the pace at which you live. Just make certain you have some rules. Here are a few ideas.

- All calls, incoming and outgoing, are limited to twenty minutes.
- Older children or children who receive high ratings on my Responsibility Index (see chapter on Responsibility) may be granted

exceptions to this rule during preselected periods of the day. This can work in reverse for children with low ratings.

- All children will hang up within one minute when requested to do so.
- Abusive or otherwise ill-mannered language used while on the phone will result in immediate termination of the conversation.
- No phone calls will be made or received after a certain hour; I suggest that 10 P.M. be the absolute cutoff time.

The denial of telephone privileges is a very strong punishment to those kids to whom phone calls are more important than breathing. You have many options; start small and see what happens.

- Cut back on the permitted length of calls. For example, if you have trouble with a messy child, limit phone calls to fifteen instead of twenty minutes.
- Establish an earlier cutoff time (9 P.M. rather than 10).
- Permit only incoming calls for a week.
- Permit only calls that are duty related (school, work, etc.)
- Make the child ask each time he or she wishes to use the phone.

If these moderate measures don't work, you may have to get tougher.

- Do not take messages for the child when he or she isn't home. Tell the caller what you are doing.
- If you decide to try to eliminate a "bad companion" from your child's life, tell the companion that you don't approve of his or her

conduct and that you don't want him or her calling. This approach can lead to your child's rebellion, so be very careful if and when you do it. You have a better chance dealing with a "bad companion" by following the hints in the chapter on Peer Pressure.

- Do not call the child to the phone even when he or she is present in the home.
- If the child uses the phone without permission, simply walk up to the phone and put your finger on the button that automatically cuts off the call.

Many children have private phones in their bedrooms. This can be a good deal provided that *certain guidelines are followed.*

- It is the child's responsibility to research the costs and report back to you concerning installation, billing and related matters.
- The child must earn the money for installation and the first month's expenses *before* being allowed to proceed.
- Make certain that the installation procedure includes a plug at the end of the cord.
- The child must have some type of regular *earned income* with which to pay his or her phone bill.
- Establish an emergency fund ($50) with part of the child's savings account that is specifically earmarked for a phone bill that is bigger than the child expected.
- If the child's overall level of responsibility is good, you may choose to lend some money to help out with a phone bill. However, don't lend the money until you've reached agreement on repayment.

- To encourage loan repayment, let the child know that you will be monitoring phone usage (how late he or she talks) until the money is repaid.
- If the child is getting in over his or her head and doesn't seem able to handle the financial responsibility, tell the phone company to disconnect the phone. Then let your child talk to the phone company about getting it reconnected. (Boy, what a lesson in reality!)

If you punish by taking away a private phone, you will hear complaints. Keep these statements handy.

- "You may have paid for the phone, but you still live in my house and I pay for that."
- "Just because you pay for your own phone doesn't mean that I quit being your parent."
- "If you used the phone wisely, I wouldn't have to stick my nose into your business."
- "If you want to enjoy the advantages of the adult world, you must demonstrate that you can act more responsibly."

Television

I personally like television. However, I don't like the way that it has become our national baby-sitter. Nor am I pleased that kids sit passively in front of the "boob tube" when they should be actively pursuing reading, writing, arithmetic and the development of their individual talents.

The quickest way to control television is with the on/off button. However, this is usually not the biggest problem. The real crunch comes when kids barrage parents with Why? Parents are quick to make reference to someone else by saying, "An article I just read said that television is bad for you." Or "The PTA said . . ." or, Heaven forbid, "Dr. Kiley said . . ." If you take the easy road by referring to someone else, you erode your own authority and your children have less respect for your values.

When you take action in restricting the use of television and receive endless complaints, you can respond, "Certain programs will not be allowed in this house."

When the kids counter by saying, "Who says?" you can answer, "I do."

Don't be afraid to evaluate television programming and, even if you aren't certain, take a stand. Become a critic.

- Sample your children's television viewing at least once a month. Even if you don't like television, know what your kids are watching.
- Stay informed about the effects of television. Material such as my newsletter, "Dr. Dan's Prescription," articles in trade magazines and material distributed by such organizations as the National Coalition on Television Violence (Box 647, Decatur, IL 62521. Write for free newsletter) will aid you in making decisions about who watches what TV programs. However, you should remain at the center of the decision. Hence, you might say, "It is my moral standards that say you shall not watch that program."
- Keep a list of censored and/or questionable shows available for quick reference. Let your children see this list and, if they are reasonable about it, explain why these shows are not permitted.
- Pay close attention to television shows that contain violence, sexual stereotypes, hidden prejudices, promiscuous sexual mores, and life situations that are portrayed in an unrealistic fashion. Be ready to jump into a lively discussion about how these things are unrealistic (from your viewpoint). In this way, you can turn a troublesome situation into a productive give-and-take.

You can reduce hassles and arguments among the children about selection of television programs by following a simple procedure.

- Take the TV listings from Sunday's newspaper and cross out all shows for the coming week that are on the censored list.
- Encourage discussion about questionable shows. You must still make the final decision.
- The oldest child, provided that his or her right has not been forfeited due to irresponsibility, gets first pick of one hour of programming. Then the next oldest chooses one hour, and so on, until each child has selected one hour of programming.
- The children continue to choose in turn, up to the number of hours you've allotted each of them. The total television time should directly correlate with the amount of active learning the children are engaged in (see the last section of this chapter).
- Give yourself leeway for many exceptions by changing the procedure if and when it bogs you down.
- The choice process should be contingent upon Mom or Dad having first choice of programs during certain time periods.

Abuse of television privileges can easily result in the loss of future privileges. Here are a couple of suggestions for how to suspend privileges.

- If a child violates the choice process in any fashion, he or she watches no television for two days; or he or she chooses last next week.

- Any arguments that don't cease after one warning result in no television for a certain period of time for the one(s) who didn't hush up after your warning.

Educational television tends to get the child involved in the program. You may wish to make certain exceptions concerning educational TV.

- Check local Public Television programming carefully. Circle shows that can be watched without counting against the child's allotted time.

The most important thing you can do in supervising your children's exposure to television is to balance the passivity of watching with active learning.

- For every hour of television watching, not counting educational programs, expect your child to engage in some active learning activity.
- Hobbies, homework, special projects, sports lessons, music lessons are a few examples of active learning.

Temper Tantrums

There must be a thousand varieties of temper tantrums, each more irritating than the other. Two-year-olds scream and stomp, 4-year-olds whine continuously, preteens have hundreds of ways of complaining and nobody has to tell you how teenage tantrums can push parents to the wall.

In one light, tantrums aren't all bad; they serve to vent frustration and help kids burn off some of the excess sugar they consume. However, many children learn that tantrums solve problems; left unaltered, this idea can be very dangerous. Children who rely on tantrums have a diminished ability to deal with the harsh realities of life, if they don't find a more appropriate way to get attention and solve their problems.

I don't advise punishment as the primary discipline technique with which to combat temper tantrums. Your primary task is to *stop the tantrum*. Eliminating temper tantrums usually means ruling out any medical cause and then implementing one or more of my PRESCRIPTIONS.

Ignoring certain tantrums works best, if you have the patience. Try stopping a tantrum using these less direct techniques.

- If you can tolerate the noise, simply walk away from a tantrum. Stay away until the noise has stopped for several minutes. Then, return and give the child attention for being quiet. This simple procedure deprives the child of an audience.
- You can bodily remove the child to a distant area and then ignore him or her as above. Be sure to move the child gently but firmly *before* you get too angry and might hurt him or her. You may say, "You'll receive no attention until you've calmed down and can play quietly."
- When you hear the angry cry (as opposed to the hurt cry) coming from your infant, ignore as in the above two hints. This is very difficult for young parents to do. Yet, someday, you must teach your loved one that screaming doesn't get anything but a sore throat.
- These hints are best used with children from infancy through about 5 or 6 years of age.

If your child's tantrum is wild or he (she) presents a danger to himself (herself), others or material things, you might have to take more direct action.

- With firm resolve, hold the wild child from behind (hands on the shoulders probably work best). Avoiding eye contact, say, "Stop it right now!"
- Place the child on a chair or stand him/her in the corner. The chair is less punitive. Remind the child that he or she must stay in the corner or on the chair until quiet. This procedure is *not* exactly the same as the one

outlined in the chapter on The Reward of Punishment because you can let the child go free after he/she has calmed down; you don't have to wait several minutes.

- Whatever technique you employ, you need not carry it any further once the child has calmed down. Remember, your primary goal is to *stop the tantrum.*

Here are more techniques you can use to stop a tantrum whether or not the child is wild.

- Make a loud noise by clapping your hands or whistling. Using this "startle," you can often interrupt a tantrum and say, "Stop it!"
- For the patient and tolerant parent—stand beside your tantruming child and simply stare at him or her. It may take several minutes before the child calms down and looks at you, wondering what you're doing. When the tantrum stops, ask the child to do something that will take his or her mind off whatever it was that got him (her) angry.

Here is an innovative technique you can try if you have a bright child who's very persistent in staging temper tantrums.

- One mother who got fed up with tantrums used this approach: When the child started a temper tantrum, the mother had a temper tantrum of her own—jumping up and down, whining and making all sorts of loud, strange noises. The child stopped his own tantrum and looked at Mom like she was nuts and said, "Cut it out, Mommy." Mom replied, "I'll quit if you will." This mother swears that it never happened again.

For older kids (say, over the age of 8 or 9), you're well advised not to argue because you'll never win. Here are a few words to use to stop the tantrum of an older child.

- "You have a right to your frustrations but I expect you to control them. I don't want to be subjected to your frustrations, I've got enough of my own."
- "Let's stop this tantrum, we're not getting anywhere."
- If you forget and catch yourself arguing, stop yourself and say, "Hey, time out! You got me going but it's over."
- In all cases, no matter what you say, after you've said it, walk away and/or ask your child to leave.

You improve your chances of preventing temper tantrums if you give the child a rewarding experience after he or she has resumed appropriate work or play.

- Timing is very important in giving attention to a child who engages in tantrums. Give the attention *after* the child has resumed appropriate activity, *not* immediately after the child quits the tantrum. In short, you want to reward the child's appropriate play, not the cessation of a tantrum. Waiting a few minutes can make a big difference in the lesson a child learns.
- The rewarding experience can be very simple: a hug, a pat on the head, a few kind words, such as, "Boy, I sure appreciate you behaving yourself. Thank you."

Toilet Problems

Children who regress in taking care of their bodily functions prove to be the undoing of many parents. I've seen young mothers, when confronted with wet and/or dirty pants, become instantly convinced that they are total failures. I try to make light of it, arguing that it certainly doesn't do any good to get so upset. But they are quick to tell me stories that are so graphic in stinky details that my heart (and nose) goes out to them.

Take charge of yourself and the situation by following these helpful hints:

- Rule out any physical problems by consulting your family doctor.
- Review the happenings in the child's life during the past few weeks and see if there is or has been any serious stress. Death, divorce or cases of abuse could be causing the problem. The older the child, the more likely that internal stress is present.

- Some toilet problems are a result of the child using wet or dirty pants to punish or manipulate you. Honestly evaluate how much yelling or screaming you do when the child has dirty pants. Your emotions could be undermining the child's toilet training.
- Consult the book, *Toilet Training in Less Than a Day*, a very popular and helpful paperback written by Drs. Nathan H. Azrin and Richard M. Foxx. If this doesn't help, seek help from a professional. One or two hours of individual consultation could help you uncover and correct small errors in your parenting.

Work and Chores

After I had given my work-and-chores presentation at a parenting conference, an older man rose and said, "It's about time we get support from a doctor for doing away with child-labor laws!" Boy, did that guy misunderstand what I said.

Just because I want our children to understand the joys and suffering of work doesn't mean that I want them to lay down their toys and pick up a shovel. In fact, too much work causes children to miss out on much of their childhood. I want kids to be goofy, playful and make childish mistakes. That's how they learn. But I also want them to have first-hand knowledge of the world of work, first through household chores and later by working in the neighborhood or as part of the teenage work force.

Parents must administrate this work so that children properly budget their time between work and play. I can't give you an exact formula to use in developing this time budget. Family financial resources, extracurricular activities and the child's need to study are a few of the things that may create exceptions to any set of rules. Use my hints as a jumping-off point in establishing a set of work standards appropriate to your situation.

I separate work into three categories, each with a special purpose.

- *Chores.* Chores around the house teach younger children the necessity of working to earn money. Older kids learn the lesson: Your commitment to family life includes helping around the house without payment.
- *Work-as-punishment.* Certain boring or menial tasks may be assigned to children as punishment.
- *Work for money.* Certain household tasks that are above and beyond regular chores can be done in exchange for payment.

Household chores should be part of every child's daily routine. When chores become habitual, a child has an easier time adjusting to other boring times.

- Chores can begin for a child when he (she) is old enough for this guideline to apply: Children are old enough to clean it up when they are old enough to mess it up.
- Chores should begin small and build in complexity and difficulty as the child matures. Here are some examples:

  For a 5-year-old. Take out the garbage, pick up his or her toys, feed the pet and put his or her clothes away.

  For a 10-year-old. Straighten up his or her bedroom daily, set and clear the table for meals, assist with weekly cleaning and any of the chores from the previous age level.

For a teenager. Clean bathroom and bedroom regularly, do part of laundry and vacuum twice weekly.

- You must always reserve the right to ask the child to help with special assignments (for example, cleaning out cupboards).
- While teaching children how to do household chores, you may elect to do many of the tasks yourself. If so, make certain the kids at least know how to do such things as work the stove, dishwasher, washer and dryer, iron and other appliances that are a part of everyday living. Children should have a working knowledge of how to prepare a meal, do the dishes and the laundry by 13 years of age.

There are times when certain kinds of work assignments serve as excellent disciplinary tools.

- If work is used as punishment, it should be menial and boring, having some relationship to a cleaner house. For example, work assignments might include scrubbing down basement steps, scrubbing out the inside of the shower, bath or toilet bowl, or polishing the garbage cans.

To keep work-as-punishment from becoming disastrous, keep a few rules in mind.

- Work assignments are most effective when used with children over the age of 10 or 11.
- For best results, assign the work in terms of a job. For example, "Your penalty is to wash down the basement steps with a brush."
- Regular chores might be used as discipline when one child has been cruel or unjust to a sibling. For example, "Because you used

your brother's radio without permission, you must do all his chores plus your own for three days."

- Once you've elected to use work-as-punishment, make the child complete the task as soon as possible. Children should receive no privileges, freedoms or other goodies until the task has been completed.
- Assign the work detail when you or another responsible adult can supervise the work. This may mean that the work penalty isn't enforced until a weekend. However, if the infraction occurs more than a day or two before the work penalty can be implemented, I prefer that you find another, more immediate punishment.
- If the child is loafing or otherwise not completing the work, threaten to add another job by saying, "You should have finished those steps by now. Get moving or else you'll have to do the porch too."
- Don't forget: the time should fit the crime. For example, if the chlid is fifteen minutes late getting home and has no good reason, you should assign a work penalty that lasts thirty minutes—fifteen minutes to make up for being late and fifteen minutes to pay you back for your worry.
- For an older and/or more responsible child, you may use a work penalty as one alternative that the child may choose in paying for his or her mistake. For example, if the child is a half-hour late getting home, and has no good reason, you might say, "You will pay for being late, but you have a choice. You can come in one hour earlier next Friday, skip television and radio for four days, or clean the walls of both bathrooms." Just

make certain that each alternative is seen by the child as painful. Don't be surprised if the child chooses the work penalty; it's okay. The sooner a punishment is over the better for everyone involved.

Work for money—kids shouldn't work forty hours a week unless they absolutely have to. But all children should learn how to work for money.

- If you recheck my PRESCRIPTIONS in the chapter on Money, you'll find that I suggest that allowances should self-destruct sometime during the teen years. After that, children should be helped to earn money on their own.
- If at all possible, help the child find a job working for someone else, even if only a neighbor. Success in working for someone other than their parents gives children an added dimension of self-confidence that will carry over into other areas (for example, school).
- If the child's age prohibits a regular part-time job, encourage him or her to work at odd jobs in the neighborhood: mow lawns, shovel snow, rake leaves, baby-sit, have a paper route or pursue any other idea that free enterprise might suggest.
- If circumstances prohibit the child from working for someone else, you should explain to the child that you will make available certain household jobs that you will pay him or her to complete. If you follow this course, keep these ideas in mind:
    1. Keep a list of jobs that you are willing to pay the child to do. Examples might be: washing and waxing the

car, cleaning out the garage, tutoring a younger sibling in reading or spelling, washing the cupboards, washing the windows or trimming the bushes. These jobs should be over and above the chores you expect the child to do without payment.

2. Be willing to negotiate a price before the job is assigned. Avoid problems of laziness by agreeing on a total price rather than an hourly rate. Assign a wage that is in keeping with your budget and what you might have to pay a handyman if he did the job.

3. Agree on a time *by which the job will be completed.* Make certain you explain exactly what you want achieved (no streaks on the windows or dirt piles in the corners.).

4. To reduce conflicts, I suggest you have the child write down the specifics of the agreement and both of you sign it.

Some kids just don't seem to learn the knack of finishing a job they started. If your child is slow to get the hang of how to finish a job correctly, try something I call "positive practice."

- Suspend all other activities and focus on one aspect of the unfinished job, let's say a small pile of dirt in one corner of the place to be cleaned (garage).
- Have the child clean up the dirt correctly (sweeping completely into a dustpan), then *have the child put the dirt back in the cor-*

ner and repeat the correct cleaning method.

- With immediate supervision have the child clean up another dirty area. Then, say, "I hope that next time you will finish the job you've started."
- *At no time* during this positive-practice procedure do you belittle, or make negatively critical remarks to the child.
- If any sibling makes fun of the child, assign a work detail to that child.

Working Parents

More and more families are learning to cope with both parents working outside the home. This outgrowth of modern living isn't necessarily damaging. In fact, it can provide the opportunity for the family to become more effective.

I trust that you work in order to provide your children with a more satisfied, fulfilled parent and greater economic security. There's certainly nothing wrong with that. Furthermore, I think you should expect your kids to help you attain the goals you've set for your family.

I support the notion of giving kids quality time when you can't give them the quantity that you and they might want. But this is not a new idea. Our grandparents who worked long, hard hours, knew the importance of quality time. And now, after passing through an era of easy living, we must rediscover the conventional wisdom that has served us so well. We can all work hard and still give our children the things that they need. It just calls for some modern PRESCRIPTIONS.

Conserve your time and energy in every way possible.

- See that you have a food freezer big enough to store five days of pre-prepared dinners. Relying upon casseroles and preset servings (individually wrapped hamburgers) can save time. Prepare your evening meals on Sunday. Expect the older children to help.
- Invest in a microwave oven and cut your dinner preparation time to under ten minutes.
- Buy simple clothing that doesn't require much maintenance.
- If you don't have a pet at the present time, it's a good idea *not* to get one.
- Establish and make regular use of a centralized message center. Leave messages of your schedule and special things for the children to remember. Require that junior and senior high students leave a message as to their whereabouts and a phone number where they can be reached.
- Children under the age of 8 or 9 should at least have a neighbor watching over them.

Use many different methods to get children involved in the care and preservation of the family.

- Let your children know that, if they get involved in many extracurricular activities, you will *not* be able to attend all the functions in which parents participate. Make every possible effort to attend the activities associated with at least one outside interest.
- Let the children see the general condition of your budget. Without placing an undue bur-

den on them, show them where the money goes. This would be applicable to kids over the age of 10.

- Get the kids used to using public transportation, bicycles and walking. They must take some responsibility for getting places.
- The older the child, the more he or she should participate in household tasks. A 6-year-old can set and clear the table, a 9-year-old can get the food out of the freezer, a 12-year-old can be in charge of dishes and a 15-year-old should be able to prepare a dinner from scratch at least once a week.
- Any child over 12 should be able to do his or her own laundry.
- If an older child is in charge of supervising a younger brother or sister, tell the older one to report minor disruption to you rather than trying to "parent" the sibling. You can take swift action when you get home as you protect the older one from being seen as a parent.

Management of problems must also reflect time and energy conservation.

- Make it *very clear* that you are to be called at work *only* in case of emergencies.
- Organize a "Job Squad" on Saturday mornings and clean your house like a white tornado.
- If you must discipline, use methods that settle the problem the same night. For example, don't ground a child for a week; rather, let bedtime come an hour or two earlier; use suspension of television *and* phone privileges for *one* night instead of television or

phone for two nights. The best penalty when two parents are working is one that is *over with* soon.

- Consider using the Merit/Demerit chart in the Appendix as your main monitoring device.

Dr. Dan's 1001st
PRESCRIPTION

- This is probably the most important hint of all. At least once a week, when your child is amusing himself or herself, approach the child and say, "I love you very much. You are very important to me." Hesitate a moment and then walk away. The first few times you do it, the child might not respond or may even think you've lost your marbles, but he or she will never turn away from the warmth contained in unconditional love.

Appendix

As many of you might know, I like graphs, charts or any other paper-and-pencil device that simplifies the difficult task of monitoring children's activity. As a bonus to the 1001 helpful hints, let me share with you the DR. DAN's MERIT/DEMERIT CHART, or as I suggest parents tell their kids, the "I'm gonna quit yelling" chart.

An example of the chart (for a fictitious 10-year-old named Joe) and some explanations should help you decide whether or not this device will help you.

This is a very simple way to add up Joe's positive and negative behaviors. The X stands for a positive behavior while the O represents a negative one. The few words under "Behavior" explain the positive and negative marks. You can use any words that you *and* the child will understand.

The chart is designed to give the child a reward or penalty when a net of 5 positives or negatives is reached. Thus, when Joe reached a negative 5 (7 O's minus 2 X's, he had to go to bed an hour earlier. The double lines

Joe's Merit/Demerit Chart

	X	O	Behavior	
10/13	X		Extra nice to grandma	
		O	Left an apple core in F.R.	
		O	Mouth	
		O	Mouth	
10/14		O	Didn't make bed	
	X		Helped sister with homework	
		O	Shoes in the hallway	
		O	Messy bathroom	
10/16		O	Forgot garbage	−5 Bed at 8P.M.

$+5$ = Extra TV
-5 = Earlier to bed

mean that once he goes to bed earlier, he is even with the board.

Let's review Joe's behavior and see what the chart represents.

> Joe got an X for being extra nice to grandma, who can be a pill.
>
> He got an O for leaving an apple core in the family room.
>
> He got an O for excessive sassing (hence, the word "Mouth").
>
> He got another O for calling his brother a "fag."

He got an O for leaving his bed a disaster.

He got an X for helping his sister with her homework.

He got an O for leaving his shoes in the hallway.

He got an O for leaving the bathroom a mess.

He got an O for failing to take out the garbage.

Here are some other hints to keep in mind if you use the chart:

- Explain to the children that you want to reduce your yelling and reminders and give them a chance to be more responsible.
- Children over age 10 or 11 may think this chart is very stupid. You can explain that you will be glad to suspend the chart *if* they become responsible.
- Implement a practice chart for several days *prior* to the real thing. This gives the kids a chance to see what's coming without getting penalized for bad habits immediately.
- You can use the chart with almost any child. It is especially useful with school-age children.
- You don't have to change the page until it is full; just keep the dates to the left so that you know how often you are using the chart.
- The child may wish to change the reward for a +5; you may wish to change the penalty for a −5. You must have final say on both rewards and punishments.
- If the child has a particularly bad day and suddenly reaches a −10, simply double the penalty. In Joe's case, he would go to bed *two* hours earlier, at 7 P.M.
- You may wish to give double X's or O's for

outstanding performance or unbelievable disruption.

- You should make a conscientious effort, especially at first, to find positive things to enter on the chart. Even a constant disrupter does some things right. If you can't find anything positive to put on the chart, you should seek professional help.
- There may be days when you do not list any positive or negative behaviors. It's just one of those neutral days.
- Save the old charts so you can see how the children are improving or going downhill over time.
- Only parents or supervising adults (baby-sitters) may use the chart. If kids mess up the chart, they receive an automatic −5.
- If the child fails in a task (taking out garbage), he or she gets an O *but still must complete the task.* If the task isn't completed in a reasonable length of time (ten minutes), give another O. Do not keep reminding the child of the task.
- Both you and your spouse should use the chart. You can compare what behaviors you each think the children should improve upon.
- If you have more than one child, I advise you to give each child his or her individual chart.
- Post the chart in a prominent place (on the refrigerator). You can put it inside the cupboard if the kids don't want their friends to see it.

You can suspend use of the chart when you rarely find something negative to mark down. I suggest you occasionally review the child's level of responsibility (see the chapter on Responsibility at the beginning of the book). If and when it improves, throw the chart away. After all, paper-and-pencil procedures are meant to self-destruct when the children demonstrate that such contrived methods are no longer necessary.

Index

Active ignoring, 58
Active learning, 228
Alcohol use, 115
  driving and, 81-82
  by parents, 119, 152
Anger, misplaced, 59-60
Authority, 29-35
  changing your mind and, 34-35
  defiance of, 33-34
  fear and, 32-33
  following through on, 30-31
  limiting alternatives in, 40
  overcoming manipulations and, 34
  responsibility and, 30
  saying No, 31-32
Automobile use, see Car privileges
Azrin, Nathan H., 234

Baby-sitters, 65-66
  for single parents, 206
Back talk, 69-70
"Bad companions," 155-56
"Bad language," 134-35
Bedtime, 72-73
Behavioral directions, 11-12
Bell, Ruth, 193
Blackmail, 93-94
Boarding school, 184
Boredom
  drug abuse and, 117-18
  as penalty, 53
Bribes, 163
Brushing teeth, 85
Budgets, 140-41
Bullying, 182-83

Car, sibling fights in, 203
Car privileges, 77-82
  cleaning the car and, 80
  for driving to school, 79
  hours per week of, 80
  while intoxicated, 81-82
  lateness and, 81
  miles per week for, 79-80
  speeding tickets and, 81

Changing Bodies, Changing Lives
  (Bell), 193, 198
Cheating, 125-30
  chronic, 129-30
  inadvertent stimulation of, 126
  overcorrection for, 128
Choices, giving children, 39-40
Chores, 235-37
Cleanliness, 83-85
Clothes, 87-90
  abuse of, 88
  failure to put away, 88-89
  for preteens and teenagers, 89
  purchasing, 89
Competition, 154
Complaints, 91-96
  blackmail in, 93-94
  materialistic, 95-96
  peer pressure and, 93
  about school, 92
  to single parents, 207
  understanding and, 94-95
  of unfairness, 92-93
Contraception, 197
Counseling, see Professional help
Credibility of parents, 37
Curfews, 73-74
Custody fights, 113

Dating, 194-95
  by single parents, 207
Day care, 65-67
Death, 97-99
Directives, following through on, 30-31
Discipline
  disagreements between parents over, 123
  spanking and, 209-10
  by working parents, 245-46
  See also Authority; Punishment
Disrespect, 69-70
Disruptive teenagers, 101-8
Divorce, 109-13
Dress code, 87, 90
  violation of, 90

255

Driving, see Car privileges
Drug abuse, 115–19

Educational television, 228
Explanation, 37–41
  honest, 38
  of new jobs, 40–41
  overdoing, how to avoid, 41
  of punishment, 52, 59
Explorations
  disruptive, 38–39
  responsibility and, 40

Families Anonymous, 206
Family dynamics, 121–23
Fear
  healthy, 32–33
  in prevention of drug abuse, 116
Fights
  between parents, 122
  between siblings, 202–4
Financial responsibility, 137–40
Foods for Healthy Kids (Smith), 76
Foxx, Richard M., 234
Freedom, restriction of, 52–53

Goldfarb, Gerald, 110
Grandparents, 122–23
Grounding, 52–53
Guilt
  parental, 19–20
  vs. regret, 60

Hair, length and style of, 90

Ignoring, 58
  active, 58
  tantrums, 230
Individuating activities, 154–55
  in prevention of drug abuse, 116

Jobs
  learning new, 40–41
  See also Work

Kübler-Ross, Elizabeth, 97, 98

Lateness
  with car, 81
  chronic, 75
  to meals, 76
  to school, 72

Limits, testing, 38–39
Living with Death and Dying
    (Kübler-Ross), 98
Loans, 141–42
Love, unconditional, 247
Lying, 125–30
  chronic, 129–30
  inadvertent stimulation of, 126
  outlandish, 127
  overcorrection for, 128

Manners, 131–35
Marijuana use, 115
  driving and, 81–82
Marks, Burton, 110
Masturbation, 194
Materialism, 59
  and complaints, 95–96
Mayle, Peter, 193
Meals
  being on time for, 75–76
  manners at, 133
  washing before, 84
Medical screening, 184
Merit/Demerit chart, 32, 246,
    250– 53
Messiness, 85–86
Mistakes
  admitting, 21–22
  restitution for, 22
Money
  budgeting, 140–41
  loans of, 141–42
  responsibility about, 137–40
  work for, 236, 239–40
Movies, sex in, 193–94
Mud, tracking in, 85
Music, 143–45

National Coalition on Television
    Violence, 226
National Institute for Alcoholism,
    Drug Abuse and Mental
    Health, 115
National Runaway Hot Line, 169
National VD Hot Line, 199
Negative Family Activity (N.F.A.),
    23
  coping with, 26
  definition of, 24
Negotiable rules, 47–48
Nocturnal emissions, 194

Nonnegotiable rules, 47
   against drug abuse, 116–17
Nonverbal communication, 32
Nuclear family, 121
Nutrition, 117

Orderliness, 85–86

Parents without Partners, 206
Partner Activity (P.A.), 24
Part-time parents, 147–50
Passive resistance, 54–55
Peer pressure, 93, 150–56
   drug abuse and, 116
Philosophy of life, 19 •
Pleasantries, common, 132–33
Popular music, 143–45
Pornography, 194
Positive Family Activity 23–27
   definition of, 23–24
   sibling rivalry prevented by, 204
   for single parents, 27
   suggestions for, 25–26
Positive partial-Family Activity
   (P.pF.A.), 24
Positive practice, 240–41
Possessions
   failure to put away, 86
   taking away, as punishment, 57
Privacy, 157–59
   violation of, 158–59
Privileges
   denial of, as punishment, 57
   of rank, 48–49
Professional help, 185–89
   evaluation of, 187–88
   how to find, 186–87
   when to seek, 186
Public disruption, 161–65
Public Television, 228
Punishment, 51–61
   boredom as, 53–54
   through denial of privileges or
      possessions, 57
   in development of authority, 31
   discipline and, 52
   explanation of, 52
   fear of, 32
   misplaced anger and, 59–60
   overexplaining, 59
   overextending, 60
   oversights that undermine, 58–60

through passive resistance, 54–55
through restriction of freedom,
   52–53
rewards and, 60–61
for stealing, 214
by taking away private phone,
   224
work as, 55, 236–39
yelling as, 56

Rank, privileges of, 48–49
Regret vs. guilt, 60
Religion, 153–54
Removal, 58
Respect for others, 133–34
Responsibility
   authority and, 30
   defined, 17
   exploration and, 40
   index for determining level of,
      17–18
   in prevention of drug abuse, 116
   review of, 252–53
   sex and, 195
Restaurants, disruptive behavior in,
   164–65
Restitution, 22
   for stealing, 214
Rewards, 60–61
   discipline and, 52
   distinguished from bribes, 163
   for improved behavior in school,
      181
Rock concerts, 145
Role reversal, 204
Rules, 43–49
   against drug use, 116–17
   as guidelines for saying No, 31
   list of, 44–45
   negotiable, 47–48
   nonnegotiable, 47
   review of, 45–46
   telephone, 221–22
Runaways, 167–69

Sadness, 171–73
School, 175–84
   boarding, 183–84
   bullying at, 182–83
   communicating with personnel of,
      176–77
   disruptive behavior in, 180–81

School (Cont.)
skipping, 181–82
special education, 184
teacher problems, 178
underachievement in, 179–80
School bus, 183
Self-control, parental, 119
Sex, 191–99
dating and, 194–95
masturbation, 194
in movies and on television,
193–94
solid information about, 192–93
in songs, 144–45
stereotyping, 192
trust about, 195
Sexually transmitted diseases
(STDs), 198–99
Sibling rivalry, 201–4
parental intervention and, 202
Positive Family Activities to prevent, 204
role reversal and, 204
Single parents, 205–7
complaints to, 207
dating by, 207
Positive Family Activities for, 27
support systems for, 205–6
Smith, Lendon, 76, 117
Snoopervision, 105–6, 158–59
Solitary Activity (S.A.), 24
Spanking, 209–10
for public disruption, 163
Special education, 184
Speeding tickets, 81
Staying up late, 75
Stealing, 211–15
Stepparents, 217–20
comparison with natural parents,
218–19
objectivity of, 219–20
part-time, 148–49
Stopping behaviors, 58
Supermarkets, disruptive behavior
in, 161–64
Supervision in prevention of drug
abuse, 118

Table manners, 133
Talking back, 69–70
Tantrums, 229–32
ignoring, 230

prevention of, 232
public, 161–65
wild, 230–31
Teenage disruption, 101–8
Teeth, brushing of, 85
Telephones, 221–24
denial of privileges, 222–23
private, in child's room, 223–24
rule for using, 221–22
Television, 225–28
active learning vs., 228
educational, 228
evaluation of, 226
messiness while viewing, 85–86
selection of programs, 227
sex on, 193–94
suspension of viewing privileges,
227–28
Temper tantrums, *see* Tantrums
Therapy, *see* Professional help
"Time out," 34
as punishment, 53–54
Toilet problems, 233–34
Toilet Training in Less Than a Day
(Azrin and Foxx), 234
Truancy, 182

Unconditional love, 247
Underachievement, 179–80
Understanding, 94–95

Values, parental, 20–21
Venereal disease, 198–99
Visits, disruptive behavior during,
165

Waking up, 71–72
"Wet dreams," 194
What's Happening to Me? (Mayle),
193
Where Did I Come From (Mayle),
193
Wild tantrums, 230–31
Winning with Your Lawyer (Marks
and Goldfarb), 110
Work, 235–41
for money, 236, 239–40
positive practice of, 240–41
as punishment, 55, 236–39
Working parents, 65, 243–46

Yelling, 56

258